William Alexander Oribello's

GODSPELLS

I wish to acknowledge special thanks to the following
people who helped me make this book a reality:

SELMER PAYNE, LORRAINE RAVENEAU, CAROL GLEATON,
DEIRDRE SCHWARTZ AND BETTY BOYD, FAITHFUL HELPERS
OF THE MYSTIC LIGHT SOCIETY. ALSO TO MY PUBLISH-
ER AND FRIEND, TIMOTHY GREEN BECKLEY OF INNER
LIGHT PUBLICATIONS.

**INNER LIGHT PUBLICATIONS,
BOX 753, NEW BRUNSWICK, N.J. 08903**

GODSPELLS by Wm Alexander Oribello
Copyright© 1986
Reissued 1997 by Inner Light Publications

NOTE FROM THE PUBLISHER

The publisher is saddened to notify Mr. Oribello's many student's that this master teacher passed to a higher plane in San Francisco at the end of 1996. He had accurately predicted his own passing and told those with close ties that he would continue to serve humanity from the next world. So there would be no accidental alterations to his work we have kept the original text in its "home spun" work book format.

FREE SUBSCRIPTION TO OUR WEEKLY NEWSLETTER
AVAILABLE AT -- WWW.CONSPIRACYJOURNAL.COM

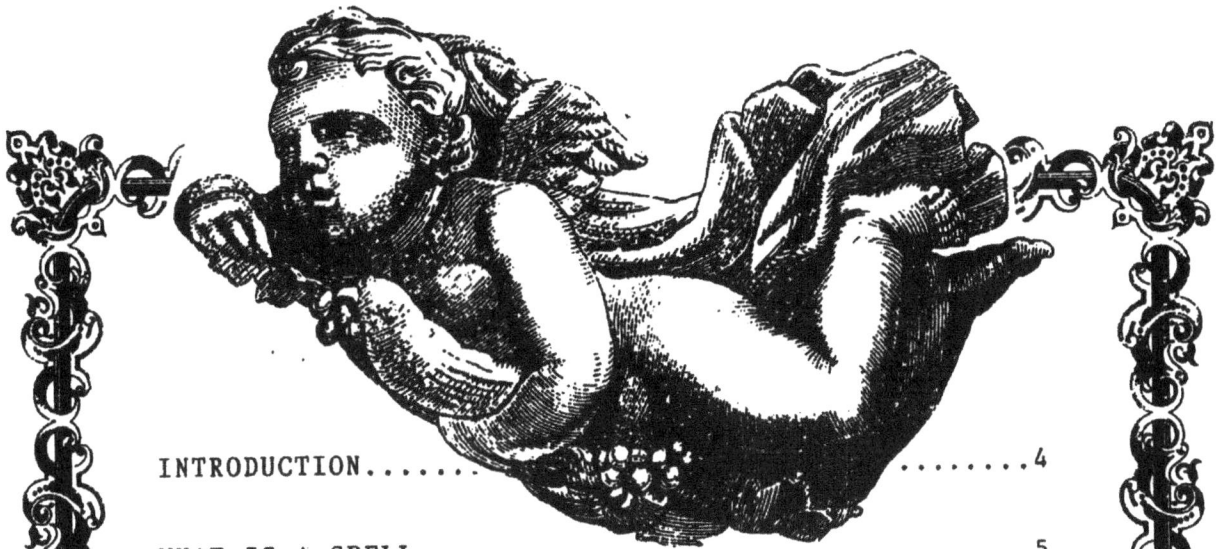

Contents

INTRODUCTION

We live in a day and age when people are beginning
to understand words like "spells" and "magic" (sometimes spelled with a 'k' as in magick, to separate it
from the common word used to describe stage illusions).
There was a time when, at the utterance of these words,
people would conjure up hideous thoughts of sinister
characters working their evil art on helpless victims.
Add to this the centuries of public brainwashing of
the masses by organized religion, and there was a time
when it was dangerous to speak of or practice such
things. Many wise ones throughout the ages were stoned,
crucified, burned and cast in prison because of their
courage to break away from mass consciousness and venture
into the secrets of nature.

Now, at the dawn of the New Age, many people are
becoming their own scientists and priests, looking to
the universe within for the answers. They now realize
that the mystical science is a great power, not of the
devil (unless it is used for evil purposes), but the
heritage of all humankind. Between the lines of sacred
scriptures such as the Holy Bible we find many cryptic
messages to establish this fact. Even the word "Gospel"
is taken from ancient words meaning "God Spell," and
with that thought I give you the gift of wisdom in
this book.

1. WHAT IS A SPELL?

To the average person, a spell is believed to be a work of evil, created and sent by a negative witch or sorcerer to harm another. However, in this document I will try to prove the fact that a spell can be good and holy, and that they have been used by righteous men and women throughout the ages, up to our present day. Furthermore, I will prove that belief in spells are not limited to superstition and ignorance, as is commonly believed, but is practiced by all people in a greater or lesser degree-even unbelievers.

DEFINITION OF A SPELL:

According to ancient mystical science, a spell is a formula of spoken or written words (or a combination of both), believed to have magical properties by virtue of its contents of strange or unknown languages, the secret names of God or angelic beings, and the effect they produced upon the practitioner and the object of the spell.

THE PURPOSE OF SPELLS:

Spells are used to banish unwanted conditions, and attract desired blessings such as personal power, love, money, good health, etc., to the practitioner, or others that he or she is helping. This of course is the purpose of good or positive spells. A negative person may learn certain secrets of life and attempt to cast a negative

spell to harm another. We do not teach this form of negative activity, as any use of this type of knowledge for egotisticle, selfish or malicious purposes will bring the negative practitioner to grips with the Universal Law of Karma which makes very sure that we reap what we sow-good or evil. Our purpose is to teach the positive applications of spells. Thus we come to understand that the power of spells is neither good or evil, it is the application of this power by the practitioner that makes it good or evil. We teach the positive application of this power for the purpose of attracting good things into our lives, and helping others. Thus we have entitled this compendium "Godspells."

WRITTEN SPELLS:

For thousands of years, people have believed in the power of written spells: there are a multitude of symbols, magical words and prayers that people of all ages have written and carried as charms for numerous purposes.

SPOKEN SPELLS:

Any group of words of which it is believed have power when spoken in a certain manner, is a spoken spell. I have a very suprising fact to share about this subject later in this chapter.

SPELL ENHANCERS:

Different objects such as candles, incense, salt, water, oil, etc., may be used in the casting of a spell. These serve to awaken inner power from within the practitioner, by the effective power of ritual.

WHY WRITTEN AND SPOKEN SPELLS WORK:

When people carry charms of symbols or words, it represents the secret wisdom that was given to human-kind in the remote past. These strange symbols contain a higher language that stimulates   · the inner conscious-ness to achieve extraordinary things. The written word likewise empower us to reach out for greater things in renewed spirit of enthusiasm.

When we speak a group of words in the form of a rit-ualistic spell, we create a powerful vibration that permeates our entire nervous system, as well as inspires our emotional and mental being.

Spoken spells should be repeated with strong emotion and conviction.Written spells should be prepared and treat-ed with reverence.

SPELLS FROM AVERAGE PEOPLE:

People of all walks of life use spells, whether they realize or believe it or not. For example, I have observed that when some people talk of undesirable things such as death, accidents, etc., they will sometimes use the term "God forbid" in their conversation. This is, in reality, a spell to prevent the negative thing they are speaking about from actually happening.

Some people, when speaking of their good fortune, will say "knock on wood." Again, this is a spoken spell to ward off any change of fortune in a negative way.

Show people have a common term they use, "break a leg." I asked a performer why one of his friends said this to him. He said that it was a customary way of performers wishing good luck to other performers. The idea was that if an entertainer got a good deal, other performers would overcome any envy they would feel for that person by verbalizing it in this term, rather than keep it inside, and thus be actually wishing success to the other-the opposite of the words which were spoken.

I have also observed that when some people compliment another, they say "God bless you" during the conversation. This is a way of overcoming any envy they may feel towards the other person, and thus avoid giving that person the look of envy, commonly known as "the evil eye."

SPELLS IN RELIGION:

All religions contain spoken and written spells in the form of prayers and blessed items. The Rosary is an enhancer, by which a person concentrates and focuses their attention on prayers which they repeat over and over again. This repitition accompanied by concentrating on one bead after another is in reality, a spell to awaken the inner consciousness to reach for God and higher in-spiration. Prayer beads and wheels are used in other forms in Eastern , and other religions, as well as in Christianity.

The various medals upon which are inscribed Latin Phrases and images of Holy characters are talismans, or

written spells, designed to focus the believer's attention on the Saint or Angel for the purpose of invoking the illustrious being to grant favors of protection, good fortune, healing, etc.

In Lord Jesus' famous Sermon on the Mount, as recorded in St, Matthew's Gospel, chapter 5, 6 and 7, he gives unmistakable formulas of words and actions for dealing with the problems of life. Also, when asked, "Lord, teach us to pray" he gave an actual spoken formula, embodied in "The Lord's Prayer."

This is the surprising fact that I promised to reveal about spoken spells-even though some misguided religious devotees condemn such practices as being all of the devil, they are in fact using this practice, ignorant of that fact because of the misinformation they receive from their leaders.

Many people find comfort each day by reading the Biblical book of Psalms, yet, little do they know that this is a book of magical sacred spells, that when used in a certain manner, can work seeming miracles. The secrets of the power of the Psalms have been used by mystics for centuries (I teach about the power of the Psalms in my book "Sacred Magic," available from Inner Light Publications).

Read on, and I will let you in on another surprising little fact.

SPELLS IN METAPHYSICAL/NEW AGE GROUPS:

Some people involved with new thought movements, may frown on teaching such as this believing that spells may be too elementary or even classify it as black magic. However, a little mental effort will prove that even such groups who feel that they are beyond these practices do in fact perform them. For example, some groups stress dynamic affirmations, decrees or mantras as a means of inner development: are not these actually spoken formulas that bring about certain vibrations in our being? Therefore, are they not spoken spells?

Many of these same people write down their affir-mations and practice looking at them for the purpose of reprogramming their subconscious mind. They may even use mandalas or ancient symbols in their work. Are these not in fact written spells?

A person can achieve mastery, where they no longer need spells, charms or any other magical practice to achieve their goals-of such are the great souls called Masters or the Supreme Magus. But until a person reaches that degree, practices such as these are progressive steps, even indispensible tools to some,in their climb towards mastery.

So, you see, dear friend, magical spells are perform-ed to some degree at all levels of consciousness. The problem is that most people are not aware of this. When one is aware of what they do, they become a dynamo of inner power.

HOW TO BENEFIT FROM THIS BOOK:

The first thing to keep in mind is that there are many types of practices for inner development and personal power. In this work I have attempted to share the ones which I feel would be of the greatest benefit to the readers of this book.

The second thing to remember is that each spell described is a magnetic operation. By that I mean that it is designed to awaken latent powerful forces within the practitioner, to help bring about the desired results. Such magnetic operations should be prepared in secrecy and with reverence. If you tell anyone what you are doing it will cause some of your energy to be drained from this work-especially if they are an unbeliever in such things. Therefore, any effort you make to prepare correctly and work secretly will be greatly rewarded. Do not do any of these things when you are angry or upset. Do not eat for a few hours before performing any practice described.

The third thing to remember is that practice makes perfection. It will do no good just to read about these things-you must practice them. I have attempted to reveal the spells that require a minimum of preparation or materials. However, some of the rituals do call for using such objects as candles , incense and other things, along with The Key of Solomon Energizer included with this book.

You will make most of the talismans yourself, except for the ones of complicated design, which I have included

in this book. You are to keep all of these things in a safe place, where they will stay clean and untouched by anyone else. Again I repeat, keep your work secret. If you must share this with anyone, be sure they are truly with you in your work and conviction.

It would be best if you have your own room to do these things, that is totally private. However, if this is not the case, do not let that stop you from doing this work: just try to arrange things when you are alone, in any room that is convenient for you. Also, any table or shelf can become your altar, so long it is clean.

Finally, and most important, remember that this work is between you and God. You are working towards a goal, so believe in its importance and keep the faith. Your success or failure depends on your constant effort and faith. Be patient-it took some time for you to become the person that you are with your strong and weak points, so allow for some time to change things-how long it takes once you begin depends on your relationship with the higher powers of life. Therefore, strive to be in harmony with all forms of life as much as possible. In some of the spells it is required that you speak unusual words; I have tried to illustrate their sounds as simply as possible, but if you still have a problem pronouncing them, then just repeat them mentally, although they are more effective when spoken aloud.

And now, I bid you good fortune as you begin your great new work.

2   THE COMPLETE RITE OF THE MAGICAL WORD "ABRACADABRA"

Although this word has become famous for its use in stage magic, it is in reality a lost word of true magic. It comes from the ancient Hebrew statement "Ha Brachab Dabarah" which, being interpreted, means "Invoke the Blessing." Although it was used by the ancient Hebrews initiated into the Secret Science of the Kabala, its origin was found to be of the ancient Magi.

This powerful word is both written and spoken, and I will give the complete rite of this powerful spell in a moment. But first, take note that it is written in three different ways, which I will explain (see figures #1, #2 & #3).

```
                    A
                  A B
                A B R
              A B R A
            A B R A C
          A B R A C A
        A B R A C A D
      A B R A C A D A
    A B R A C A D A B
  A B R A C A D A B R
A B R A C A D A B R A
```

FIGURE #1.

This is the most popular way that it is used. However, the other two figures will reveal its other manifestations and each of the three are for a specific purpose.

```
A B R A C A D A B R A
  B R A C A D A B R A
    R A C A D A B R A
      A C A D A B R A
        C A D A B R A
          A D A B R A
            D A B R A
              A B R A
                B R A A
                  R A A
                    A
```

FIGURE #2

```
A B R A C A D A B R A
A B R A C A D A B R
A B R A C A D A B
A B R A C A D A
A B R A C A D
A B R A C A
A B R A C
A B R A
A B R
A B
A
```

FIGURE #3

I will now reveal the use of the sacred and powerful spell word in each of its three forms.

Figure #1 should be used to attune with the Cosmic Mind (God) for more wisdom, power , guidance and help in all matters of life. You should write the word out in block letters as illustrated, working from the bottom up. In other words, you print the complete word, then directly above it you print it again leaving out the last letter. You continue this, leaving out the last letter until only the A is left.

After you have written your spell, speak the complete word out loud. The 'A' is always pronounced like
the a in cat. Then repeat the word again, only this
time you leave the last letter out, and so forth, until
you only speak the letter a. While speaking this word
you should think that each time you do so you are going
deeper within your inner consciousness, and more in
tune with the Universal Mind. When you are finished,
burn the paper upon which you have written the word, and
throw the ashes outside of your house. This is symbolic
of your spell becoming a burnt offering and scattering
the ashes to the winds to be carried into the spiritual
kingdom. Repeat this as often as you wish to attune to
God, and remember, God answers our prayers in many ways;
try to be aware of omens, dreams and flashes of inspiration to help you find the guidance and blessing you ask.

Figure #2. is believed to remove illness by God's
power, according to our faith. You should print the
complete word, and continue writing it, working from
the top, going down and sideways, as in the illustration.
Be sure to leave out the last letter each time you print
the word. Then repeat the word over and over, leaving
out the last letter every time you do so until you come
to the letter a. While doing this, think that the illness is being diminished each time you say the word
leaving out a letter.

Figure #3. is said to invoke the Divine Presence
to descend into our mundane lives and help us banish

negative conditions, such as psychic attacks, the evil
eye, etc., that have been directed against us by negative people. Write the complete word, working from the
top down in the perfect shape of an upside down triangle.
This is symbolic of God reaching into our lives, in this
case. Repeat the word over and over as you have done in
the other spells. Always burn the papers after you finish
with all three spells, with one exception; when using
this third figure, do not scatter the ashes to the winds.
Wash the ashes down the drain of the sink, or flush them
down the toilet. This manner of disposing the ashes in
water only applies tó this third spell.

3 POWERFUL ABRACADABRA TALISMANS:

You may want to make the three figures of this
powerful word into three potent talismans, as many of
the wise ones have done. If you desire to do this you
must prepare all three talismans at once. Figure #1. is
for inner power; Figure #2. is for attracting good health;
Figure #3. is for protection against eathbound entities,
curses from negative people, etc.

Place all three talismans together-keep them in
a cloth bag or plastic, and wear them on your person.
Mystics who use this spell in the form of the three
talismans usually make new talismans every nine days
(they begin wearing the new set on the tenth day), after
they burn the old set. In this case you should dispose
of the ashes of the three burnt talismans all in running
water.

3 BEAUTY SPELL

This powerful spell is believed to help one become beautiful. Let us always keep in mind that true beauty is an inner thing as well as an outer asset. To become beautiful means to develop a pleasant personality, a radiant magnetism, as well as to improve our outer appearance. These things take time to develop, as we must renew many factors within our being at all levels. So, be patient and constant in your efforts.

You will have to use the Key of Solomon Energizer included with your book for this, as well as some of the other spells. Keep this energizer clean and safe. When you place candles or incense at the different points of this symbol, make sure they are in proper holders, burners, etc., so as not to damage this powerful tool. You are to place this on your altar when requested to do so. It would be wise to seal your energizer in laminating plastic, which you can buy at any good stationary store.

For this spell, you will also need a red and blue candle, and spring water (you can purchase this at most grocery stores).

Arrange the items on your Key of Solomon Energizer according to instructions in Figure #4. Dim the lights, ignite the candles, and proceed with the spell as described.

FIGURE #4.

Blue
candle

Small jar of
spring water

Red
Candle

YOUR
LEFT
SiDE

YOUR
RiGHT
SiDE

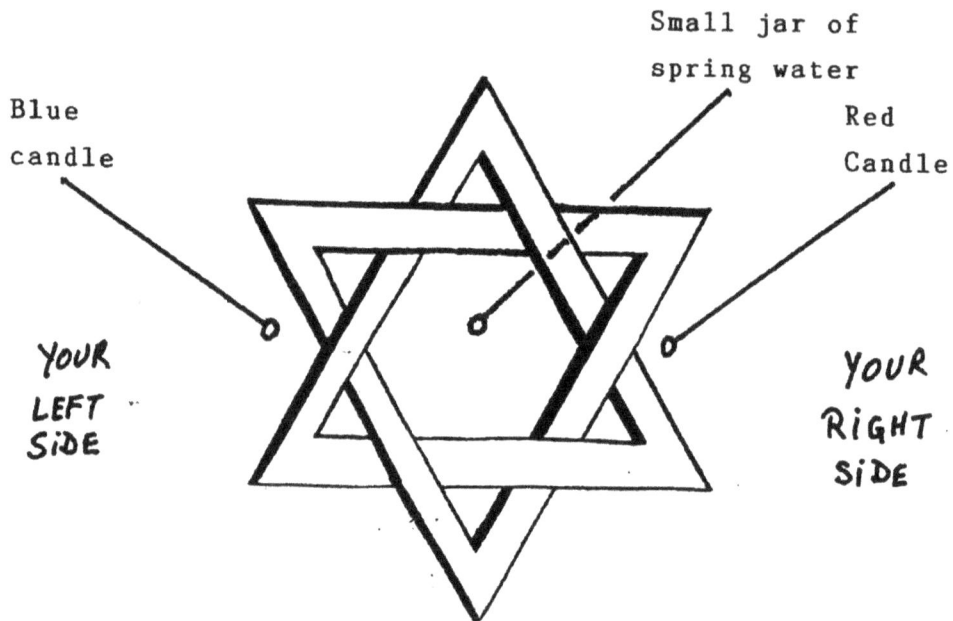

Gaze upon the candle flames and the jar of spring
water for about ten minutes. Then, close your eyes and
form a mental picture of yourself as most beautiful in
every way. Do this for fifteen minutes or so. Open your
eyes and gaze at the altar again for several minutes.
Close your eyes again and recreate your mental image of
complete beauty. Hold this image for as long as you can.
Open your eyes and repeat the following words.

"INNER BEAUTY COME TO ME, LET ME BE AS I SHOULD BE.
OUTER BEAUTY COME TO ME, VISIBLE FOR ALL TO SEE."

Repeat these words a total of seven times. When you speak, use emotional force so that you feel every word vibrating your entire being. After the spoken spell, drink the spring water. If performed correctly, this spell will charge the water with a super-abundance of magnetic energy, that you will be able to feel as you drink it. Perform this ritual as often as you like, and according to your faith so may you become.

4 CONQUERING SPELLS

These spells have been designed to help one overcome negative people who wish you harm, evil spirits,
bad luck, fear, negative thoughts, etc. Understand and
practice them well, and you will become free of all
negativity.

SPELL TO CONQUER FEAR:

Fear is a negative force that keeps many people
from attaining the great blessings of life. There is
a fear about every negative thing one can imagine;
failure, death, illness, poverty, love, family- you name
it, most people are afraid of something. Here is a
powerful spell to overcome fear.

First you must pray to God with all your heart, ask-
that the fear be removed. Talk to God as you would a
trusted friend. Then, open your Holy Bible to the 23rd.
Psalm and read it out loud with feeling. Next you must
write it on a sheet of paper, then read it out loud
again. Finally, wad the paper up in a small ball and
burn it. As it burns think that your prayer is ascending
in the smoke. Scatter the ashes to the winds.

SPELL TO OVERCOME WICKED PEOPLE:

Perhaps you are troubled by wicked people who seek
to make trouble for you in some way; through slander,
gossip, causing trouble in your home or on the job.

At times, these may be members of our own family or even supposed friends. They may say or do things to spite us, insult or make us feel inferior, undermine our plans in different ways. To overcome these people in any type of situation, perform the following spell: Purchase a "John the Conquerer Root." Have a small sheet of paper ready, as well as a black and white candle. You must arrange these items on your Key of Solomon Energizer (see figure #5).

FIGURE #5.

Black
Candle

White
Candle

YOUR LEFT
SiDE

YOUR RIGHT
SiDE

John the
Conquerer
Root

Paper

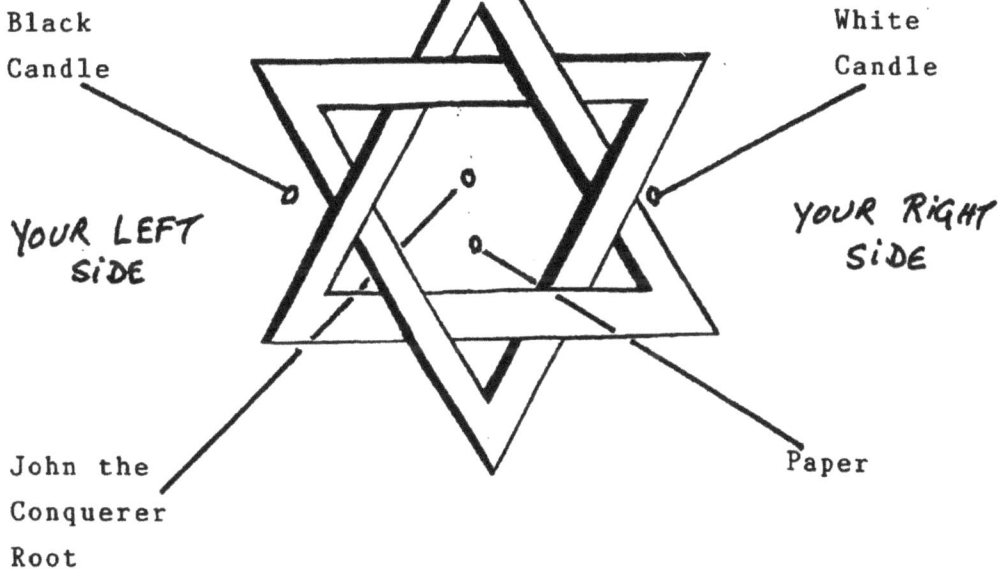

On the sheet of paper you must write the following words:

DULLIX, IX, UX. YES, YOU
ARE POWERLESS TO COME OVER
PONTIO; PONTIO IS ABOVE
PILATO. ✝ ✝ ✝

After writing these words place it on your Energizer, light the candles, make sure other lights are
dim. Gaze at the items for several minutes. Then, close
your eyes and mentally see yourself as a powerful person
with a strong mind. See your enemies confused, by reason
of your powerful magnetic shield of protection against
their cunning. Do this for several minutes until you feel
your inner power building.

Wrap the John the Conquerer Root in the sheet of
paper on which are written the words above. Carry this
with you at all times-you have just created a powerful
talisman to overcome negative people. You can use tape
to keep the paper wrapped around the root. When someone
is trying to intimidate you in any way, touch the talisman in a way that will not be noticed while looking at
them (if they are not in your presence while you are
touching the talisman, just think of them).

SPELL TO CONQUER CROSSED CONDITIONS & EVIL SPIRITS:
If you are being attacked by evil spirits in any
way, or are the victim of the negative application of
psychic energy sent to you by an evil person, perform
the following ritual:

You will use the Mystic Seal of Protection (see figure #6) of which I have included with your book.

FIGURE #6.

You will also use the Key of Solomon Energizer. Secure the following items: A small sheet of paper, a red and a purple candle, and Uncrossing Brand Incense. On the sheet of paper, write the following inscription:

I.

N I.R

I.

SANCTUS SPIRITUS

I.

N I.R

I.

ALL THIS BE GUARDED
HERE IN TIME, AND THERE
IN ETERNITY.

Arrange all items as illustrated in figure #7:

FIGURE #7.

Red
Candle

Purple
Candle

YOUR LEFT
SIDE

YOUR RIGHT
SIDE

Mystic Seal
of Protection

Paper with
inscription
and incense.

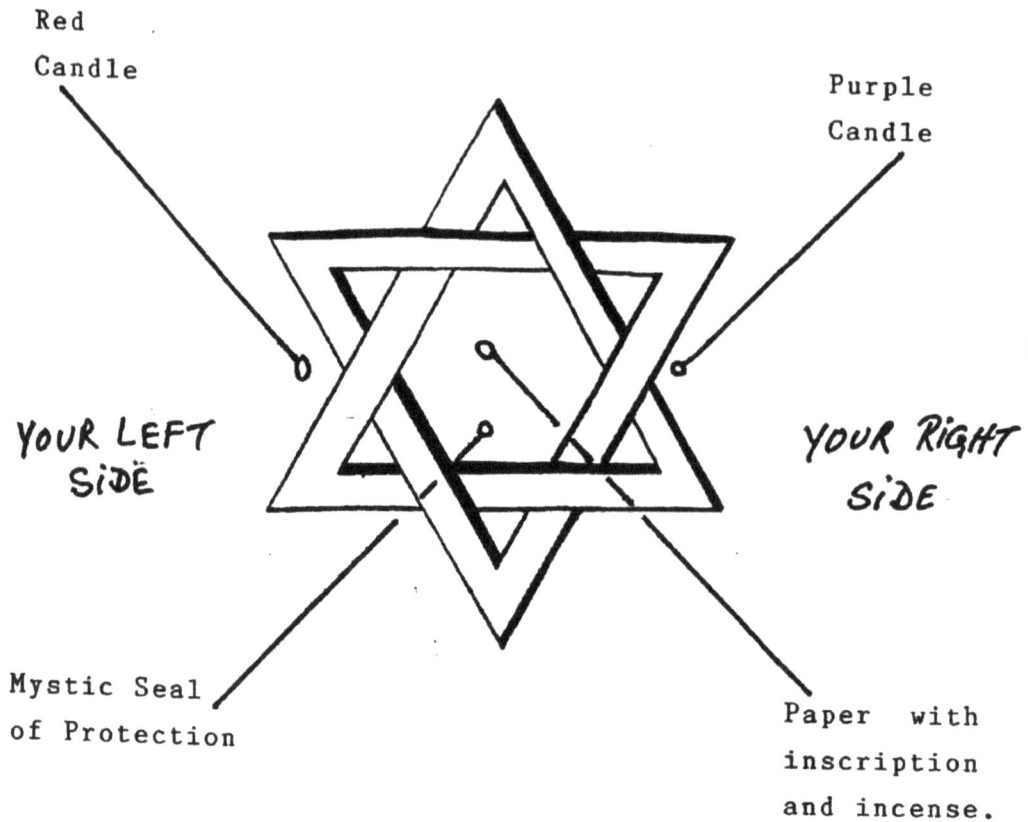

Heap a generous portion of the Uncrossing Incense
on the paper upon which you have written the special
I.N.R.I. inscription. Fold the paper and place in a metal
bowl or large incense burner. Ignite this paper and incense, light the candles and begin. Have your Holy Bible
opened to the 91st. Psalm.

Gaze at the items for several minutes. Then close
your eyes and mentally see yourself released from all

evil influences. Do this for several minutes then open
your eyes and read the 91st. Psalm with feeling in your
voice. When you have finished reading, pick up the
Mystic Seal of Protection and place it in your Bible at
the 91st. Psalm. Close the Bible and leave the seal in
it overnight-keep it close to you while you sleep. On
the next morning, open the Bible remove the seal and
start wearing it on your person.

Scatter the ashes from burning the paper and
incense to the winds.

SPELL TO CONQUER NEGATIVE THOUGHTS:
It has been said, "thoughts are things." Therefore,
we must keep this fact before our conscious when we are
tempted to think negative. Some people are greatly
troubled by negative thoughts that persist in their
draining presence within the person's mind. These can be
negative thoughts about other people or ourselves.

We can overcome negative thoughts by burning
3 Kings Brand Incense as often as possible. Also we
should always have some cloveer herb nearby, because it
has been found that if a person with a troubled mind
holds some of this herb in their left hand, they will
be relieved from their negative thoughts. The success
of this, as well as any other spell, depends on constant
practice if needed, until full success is experienced.
The altruistic statement declares that "practice makes
perfect,' and I have found this to be a fact.

SPELL TO CONQUER A STROKE OF ACCIDENTS AND PHYSICAL HARM:

Should you find that you are having too many accidents that are causing you physical harm in any way, do the following things;

Obtain three pieces of Mandrake Root. Keep one on your person at all times (when you go to sleep, keep it under your pillow).

Keep one piece hidden in the north side of your house, and the other in the east side. Hide them in places where they will not be discovered by anyone.

Many people carry this root as a charm of prevention against physical harm and illness.

A warrior cutting off the heads of the great Beast, symbolic of the power of good conquering evil.

5 DEVELOPING SPELL

There are many different methods to develop psychic
awareness. The one I am about to reveal is one that has
been highly regarded by mystic adepts. It is excellent
for helping advanced psychics become stronger, as well
as aiding the beginner in their development.

Obtain a blue candle and Sandalwood Incense. You will
also use the Mystic Seal of Psychic Development, also
called the 5th. Pentacle of Jupiter (see figure #8).

FIGURE #8

Arrange these three items on your altar, as illustrated in figure #9.

FIGURE #9.

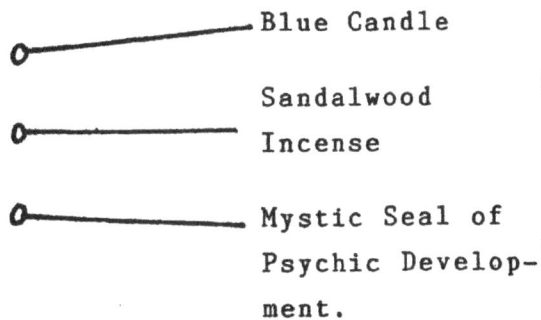

Blue Candle

Sandalwood
Incense

Mystic Seal of
Psychic Develop-
ment.

Ignite the candle and incense, dim all other lights.
Gaze at the candle flame for several minutes. Then pick
up the seal and hold it between the thumb and first finger of the left hand. Slowly pass the seal through the
smoke of the incense, back and forth, away from you and
towards you. Do this for several moments. Then hold the
seal between the palms of both hands and continue gazing
at the candle flame. After several minutes have passed
close your eyes, then begin chanting the word "OM" at
least seven times. The correct way to do this is to take
a deep breath, and as you exhale chant the word. The 'O'
is pronounced as in moon. You may repeat this spell as
often as you like and at any time you will have privacy.

Many Master Magians, such as the legendary Merlin, used
holy spells like the ones you now possess.

6 GOOD FORTUNE SPELL

If you have been unlucky in matters of the heart, business, or just about any situation in life, perform the following spell:

Take the Mystic Seal of Good Fortune, which I have included with your book (see figure #10). Open your Holy Bible to the 27th. Psalm. Hold the talisman in your right hand while you read the Psalm out loud. Place the talisman on that page after you have finished reading, and close the Bible. Now, take a penny and hold it tightly in your left hand while you make a wish. Keep the penny with you, but separate from the rest of your money, for nine full days. You are to keep the Mystic Seal of Good Fortune in the closed Bible during these same nine days. On the tenth day throw the penney away with your right hand (this is symbolic of making the conscious effort to get rid of your ill fortune). Do not throw the penny in the streets, for if someone picks it up they may receive some of the negative vibrations that held you back, and you do not wish to be responsible for this. So, throw it in a river or sewer. After you return home, take the talisman from the Bible with your left hand, and keep it with you always from that day forward. Try to keep it in your pocket, purse or on your person, on the left side as much as possible. When you need power to help your fortune, touch that area with your right hand. Again, the more secrecy you maintain, the better.

You may repeat this spell from time to time, if you feel that you need a new change in fortune. Just begin over again by placing the talisman in the Bible, using a new penny for the new spell.

FIGURE #10

IF YOUR MIND
CAN CONCEIVE IT....

AND YOUR HEART
CAN BELIEVE IT....

THEN YOUR HANDS
WILL RECEIVE IT....

A great soul

7 HEALTH SPELL

Good health is a prized possession, for without it, we can never enjoy love, money or the other good things of life. The instructions given here are not intended to substitute for a qualified physician. However, the ancients believed that one should perform spells, rituals and magickal rites for good health, as well as any other blessing. They usually employed the use of talismans and mantrums (a mantrum is a spoken spell or affirmation of a positive character and influence). Such a spell is now revealed here.

First, hold the Mystic Seal of Good Health, which I have included with your book, in your left hand. Then repeat the following spoken formula:

> I AM A RADIANT UNIT OF HARMONY AND
> POWER, THERE IS NO PLACE FOR ANY
> OTHER.
>
> SICKNESS BE GONE, HEALTH
> COME NEAR, NO CONDITIONS
> WILL I FEAR.
>
> I AM A RADIANT UNIT OF HARMONY AND
> POWER, THERE IS NO PLACE FOR ANY
> OTHER.

Keep the Mystic Seal of Good Health on your person (see figure# 11). If you   suffer   from any definite illness, rub the seal on the area after you speak the powerful mantrum, and according to your faith, so be it unto you.

FIGURE #11

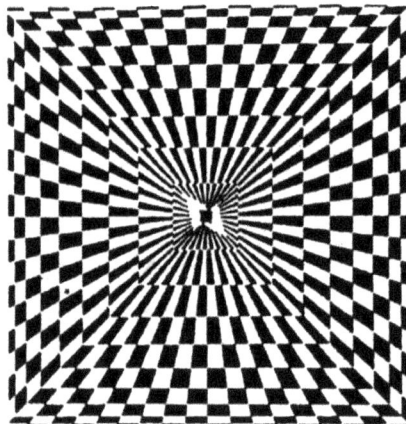

Repeat the powerful spoken spell often, as you visualize yourself radiantly healthy. This potent spell activates the cosmic forces of good health to manifest in your everyday life. It also enhances your other efforts.

You must help this spell to manifest its ultimate benefits by caring for your body through exercise, good food, relaxation, etc.

Remember, good health is everything, for without it, nothing else matters.

8 POWER SQUARE SPELLS

The legendary Power Squares have been handed down through the ages, as part of the most powerful magic on this planet. However, according to my knowledge, there is no modern day book that gives specific instructions for their correct use, except the book you are now reading. Most of the modern material I have seen only advises one to wear these as talismans. However, according to the instruction I have received, there are positive rites connected to these squares, that must be performed to release their power for the good of the practitioner. Some of the old books that have come down to us contain complex rites, which were intended to confuse the profane. This section will contain simplified rites, as they were really performed by initiates of the past.

This one section alone may be classified as a dictionary of mystic techniques in its own right, for there is a spell for just about every need.

You will prepare each square on a small sheet of paper, according to the illustrations which follow.

You will activate each square, using your Key of Solomon Energizer, and the proper color candles as instructed. You must then place the described incense on the paper, fold it up and burn it. Therefore, you must prepare the square each time you perform the same spell.

The following step by step instructions compose the prescribed ritual to activate all of the Power Squares.

1. Draw your chosen square on a plain small sheet of paper, exactly as it is in the illustration.

2. Obtain the suggested incense and colored candles for each specific spell.

3. Set up all items on your Key of Solomon Energizer, exactly the same way for each of the Power Square spells. I have illustrated this in figure #12. The only thing you would change is the color candles and the incense according to the chosen spell.

4. Always burn the prescribed incense after wrapping it in the square-and throw the ashes outside your house. Of course, you must take care that no one is watching you do this. In some cases, you may be instructed to make two squares-one to burn, and the other to use in some way.

5. Repeat the spells as often as you need to-these things must be renewed from time to time.

6. Perform only one spell at a time. If you have several needs, perform one spell, then wait until the next day if possible to perform the next one.

7. Use feeling and will power in this work.

FIGURE #12

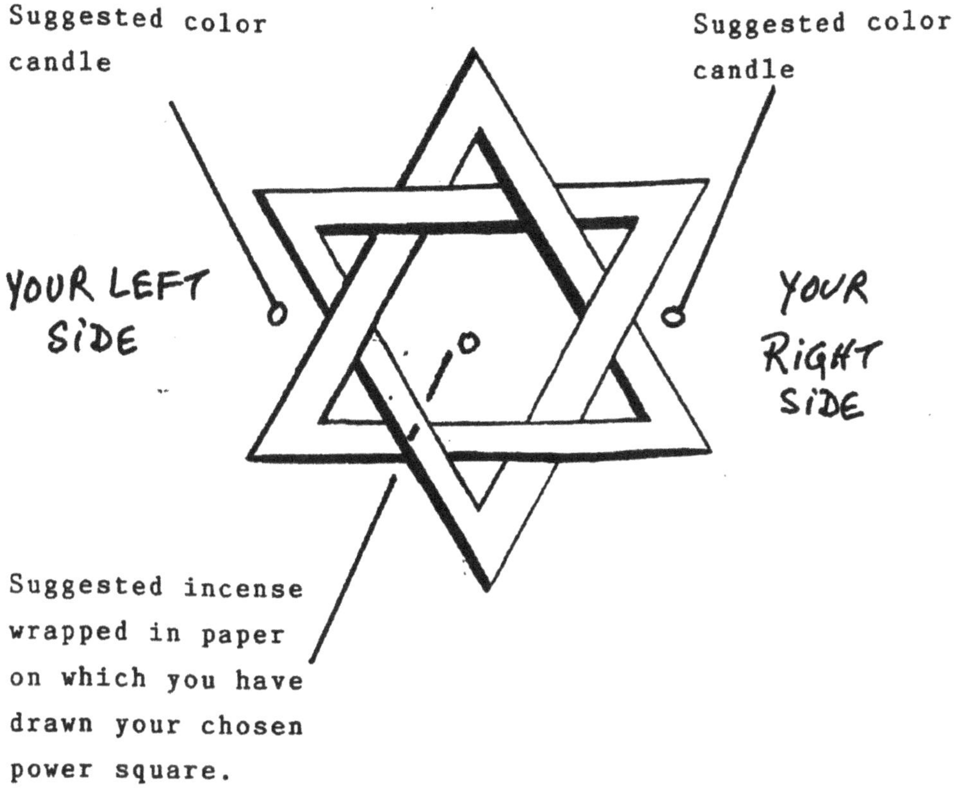

Suggested color
candle

Suggested color
candle

YOUR LEFT
SIDE

YOUR
RIGHT
SIDE

Suggested incense
wrapped in paper
on which you have
drawn your chosen
power square.

And now, I bid you God's blessings as you embark
on this wonderful journey into the magickal world of
Power Square Spells. Remember, take this work seriously.
Show reverence for this time tested power which, in the
past, was limited in its distribution, but is now made
available to you by the inspiration and guidance of our
brothers and sisters of light in the higher dimensions
of life.

FIGURE #13   THE POWER SQUARE OF SOUND BUSINESS
               (ALSO KNOWN AS THE TABLE OF JUPITER).

22	47	16	41	10	35	4
5	23	48	17	42	11	29
30	6	24	49	18	36	12
13	31	7	25	43	19	37
38	14	32	1	26	44	20
21	39	8	33	2	27	45
46	15	40	9	34	3	28

This should be burned when one needs guidance in any business decision. It is also said to be of great benefit before taking a trip to another country. Its other powers include helping one change their lives according to a religious conviction, and help in legal cases.

In addition to these, many believe in the power of this table to attract good fortune.

A red candle should be on the right side, a green candle on left. Good luck Incense is suggested.

FIGURE #14   THE POWER SQUARE OF INTELLIGENCE
              (ALSO KNOWN AS THE TABLE OF MERCURY).

8	58	59	5	4	62	63	1
49	15	14	52	53	11	10	56
41	23	22	44	48	19	18	45
32	34	38	29	25	35	39	28
40	26	27	37	36	30	31	33
17	47	46	20	21	43	42	24
9	55	51	12	13	54	50	16
64	2	3	61	60	6	7	57

This should be burned when one needs more intelligence to learn difficult things. A yellow candle should be used on both sides of the energizer, Temple Incense is suggested.

It is also believed that this seal gives protection when travelling. In both uses, one should make an extra copy to carry on their person. Whenever the spell is renewed, the old seal must be discarded for a new one.

FIGURE #15   THE POWER SQUARE OF LOVE
               (ALSO KNOWN AS THE TABLE OF VENUS).

4	14	15	1
9	7	6	12
5	11	10	8
16	2	3	13

This should be burned when one seeks to attract
that special someone, or to keep a present love. In the
latter case, one should always say "if it be God's will,
let so and so stay with me"–never try to hold a love
against their will by magic. Only pray that it be so if
it is supposed to be.

A red candle should be on the right side, a pink
one on the left. Love Attraction Incense should be
used.

FIGURE # 16   THE POWER SQUARE OF TELEPATHY

$$19254$$
$$96533$$

It is strongly believed that this square will help
one to send their thoughts to another by performing
the spell as follows;

1. Write out the square, while thinking of the person
you wish to influence, and the thought you wish to send
(do not use this knowledge for any selfish or negative
purposes).

2. Read the numbers, one row at a time out loud, then
turn your head quickly to the left.

3. Read it six more times (atotal of seven times), turning
your head in the opposite direction than the last reading. In other words, you read it the first time and turn
your head to the left then the second time you turn your
head to the right, and so forth. Finally, you burn it,
using Master Incense. A purple candle should be at the
right, a white candle to the left.

FIGURE #17   POWER SQUARE TO OVERCOME EVIL EYE

K	A	D	A	K	A	T
A	R	A	K	A	D	A
D	A	R	E	M	A	K
A	K	E	S	E	K	A
K	A	M	E	R	A	D
A	D	A	K	A	R	A
T	A	K	A	D	A	K

    If you suffer from frequent headaches and dizziness, you should first consult a qualified physician. However, if nothing is medically wrong, it could be that you are a victim of the "evil eye" or gaze of malice from a person who wishes you harm. In such a case, this square should be made and burned while you pray sincerely for help.

    A white candle should be on both sides of the energizer. Uncrossing Incense should be used.

FIGURE #18   POWER SQUARE TO DISCOVER CROSSING

H	O	R	A	H
O	S	O	M	A
R	O	T	O	R
A	M	O	S	O
H	A	R	O	H

   If you feel that your ill fortune is being caused
by someone having cast a negative spell upon you (also
known as crossing, or crossed conditions), you can know
for sure; burn this square while turning your head to
the left nine times. By that time you will get a flash
thought that it either is or is not a crossed condition.
Always remember that if our vibrations are high, no such
condition can trouble us. But, if you have one, the next
spell will help you.

   A white candle should be used on both sides of
the energizer. Temple Incense should be used.

FIGURE #19   POWER SQUARE OF UNCROSSING

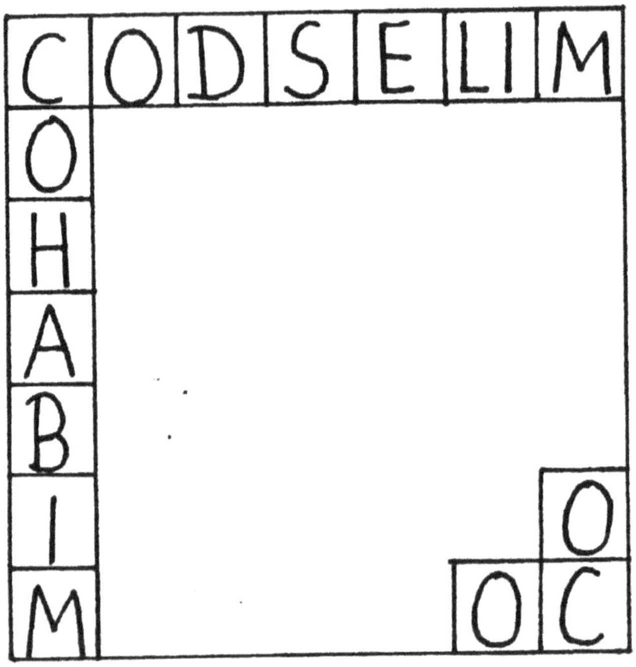
C O D S E L I M
O
H
A
B
I
M
O
O C

You must first draw the square, then wear it for nine days. On the tenth day, burn it while praying with all your heart. In your prayers, mention the names of Michael the Archangel, Blessed Mary, and Jesus the Christ.

A white candle should be used on the right side, a black candle on the left. Uncrossing Incense should be used.

FIGURE #20   POWER SQUARE TO BIND AN ENEMY

M	A	C	A	N	E	H
A	R	O	L	U	S	E
D	I	R	U	C	U	N
A	L	U	H	U	L	A
S	E	R	U	R	O	C
U	N	E	L	I	R	A
L	U	S	A	D	A	M

If someone is trying to hinder or cause you harm in any way, draw two copies of this square. Burn one while holding the other in your right hand, and think of the person. Then go and place the square you were holding, in a manner and in a place where you know the other person must walk over. This will bind them so they cannot hinder you any longer.

A purple candle should be on the right side, a white candle on the left. Master Incense should be used.

FIGURE #21 POWER SQUARE OF SECOND SIGHT

M	I	L	O	N
I	R	A	G	O
L	A	M	A	L
O	G	A	R	I
N	O	L	I	M

Burn this if you desire to enhance your extra sensory perception. You must draw two copies of this square.
Burn one while holding the other in your left hand.
Keep the one you were holding with you at all times, and
when you want to know something, past-present-or future,
hold it to your forehead at the spot between your eyebrows and pray sincerely. Be open to the subtle impressions you receive.

A white candle should be on the right side, a blue
candle on the left. Temple, or Sandalwood Incense
should be used.

FIGURE #22   POWER SQUARE OF YOUTH

```
D I S A K A N
I R O Q
S       Q
A Q
K U Q
A
N
```

It was (and still is) believed by inner circle
mystics, that to burn this square often renews one's
youth. While it is burning, you must visualize yourself younger than you are. It would be helpful for you
to place an older photo of yourself on your altar during
the ritual.

A red candle should be on the right, an orange
on on the left. Temple Incense should be used.

FIGURE #23   POWER SQUARE OF FRIENDSHIP

Q	E	B	H	I	R
E	R	A	I	S	A
B	A	Q	O	L	I
H	I	O	L	I	A
I	S	L	I	A	C
R	A	I	A	C	A

Do you wish to be highly regarded by all people?
Then burn this square as often as you can, and you
will develop your true inner beauty-for this is what
makes people feel attracted to you-for you to become
the nice person that everyone likes.

A pink candle should be used on both sides.
Temple Incense should be used.

9   ZODIAC SPELLS

Every person is born into the planetary influences, known in the study of Astrology as "the Signs of the Zodiac." There is a way that we can make the most of the energies granted to us at birth, by the use of Zodiac Spells. A Zodiac Spell is enhanced by the possession of our proper birth stone. You can wear your birth stone in a ring, neck chain, or even carry it unmounted on your person. Following is a list of the Twelve Signs of the Zodiac, along with their specific birthstones and spoken spells.

INSTRUCTIONS FOR ALL ZODIAC SPELLS:

These instructions are for all signs of the zodiac, the only thing being individual to you being your sign. Obtain the proper birthstone, hold it between the palms of your hands and repeat the specific spell. You may do this with a stone you already have, or purchase a new one. You should repeat the spell regularly (your choice of monthly, quarterly, or annually on your birthday). Speak the words with strong will power. According to the information I have received, these spell are designed to bring you the best potential for good fortune, drawing from the energies through which you were born into this dimension.

For further information on the different signs, you can read general books on Astrology.

ARIES: March 21st.-April 19th.
Birthstone-Diamond.

SPELL:

        "I, WHO FROM ARIES DATE MY YEARS,
        USE THE DIAMOND TO SHIELD ME
        FROM TEARS, AND ILL FORTUNE. I
        DECREE THAT THROUGH THIS STONE,
        ALL MY POWERS WILL BE KNOWN."

TAURUS: April 20th.-May 20th.
Birthstone-Emerald.

SPELL:

        "I, WHO FIRST BEHELD THIS
        LIFE IN THE LOVELY SPRING,
        WILL RENEW IN ALL THINGS.
        I DECREE THAT THROUGH THIS
        STONE, ALL MY POWERS WILL
        BE KNOWN."

GEMINI: May 21st.-June 20th.
Bithstone-Agate.

SPELL:

        "I, WHO CAME WITH SUMMER
        THINGS, THROUGH THE AGATE
        GOOD LUCK BRING. I DECREE

             THAT THROUGH THIS STONE,
             ALL MY POWERS WILL BE KNOWN."

CANCER: June 21st.-July 23rd.
Birthstone-Ruby.

SPELL:

             "I, WHO UNDER CANCER WAS BORN,
             WITH THE RUBY WILL ADORN.
             I DECREE THAT THROUGH THIS
             STONE, ALL MY POWERS WILL
             BE KNOWN."

LEO: July 24th.-August 23rd.
Birthstone-Sardonyx.

SPELL:

             "I, WHO UNDER LEO WAS BORN,
             WITH THE SARDONYX WILL ADORN.
             I DECREE THAT THROUGH THIS
             STONE, ALL MY POWERS WILL
             BE KNOWN."

VIRGO: August 24th.-September 22nd.
Birthstone-Sapphire.

SPELL:

> "I, WHO THROUGH VIRGO CAME,
> WEAR THE SAPPHIRE TO WIN
> GAIN, MATERIAL & SPIRITUAL.
> I DECREE THAT THROUGH THIS
> STONE, ALL MY POWERS WILL
> BE KNOWN."

LIBRA: September 23rd.-October 22nd.
Bithstone-Opal.

SPELL:

> I, WHO IN AUTUMN CAME INTO
> THIS LIFE, THROUGH THE OPAL
> WIN OVER   FEAR AND STRIFE.
> I DECREE THAT THROUGH THIS
> STONE, ALL MY POWERS WILL
> BE KNOWN."

SCORPIO: October 23rd.-November 21st.
Birthstone-Topaz.

SPELL:

> "I, WHO UNDER SCORPIO WAS BORN,
> WITH THE TOPAZ WILL ADORN.
> I DECREE THAT THROUGH THIS
> STONE, ALL MY POWERS WILL
> BE KNOWN."

SAGITTARIUS: November 22nd.-December 21st.
Birthstone-Turquoise.

SPELL:

        "I, WHO CAME IN 'SAGITTARIUS,
         DO CLAIM ALL OF THIS LIFE'S BEST.
         I DECREE THAT THROUGH THIS STONE,
         ALL MY POWERS WILL BE KNOWN."

CAPRICORN: December 22nd.-January 20th.
Birthstone-Garnet.

SPELL:

        " I, WHO IN CAPRICORN WAS BORN,
          WITH THE GARNET WILL ADORN.
          I DECREE THAT THROUGH THIS
          STONE, ALL MY POWERS WILL
          BE KNOWN."

AQUARIUS: January 21st.-February 18th.
Birthstone-Amethyst.

SPELL:

        "I, WHO CAME IN AQUARIUS, DO
         CLAIM POWER OVER THINGS AMISS.
         I DECREE THAT THROUGH THIS
         STONE, ALL MY POWERS WILL
         BE KNOWN."

PISCES: February 19th.-March 20th.
Birthstone-Bloodstone.

SPELL:

     "I, WHO IN PISCES WAS BORN,
      WITH THE BLOODSTONE WILL
      ADORN. I DECREE THAT THROUGH
      THIS STONE, ALL MY POWERS
      WILL BE KNOWN."

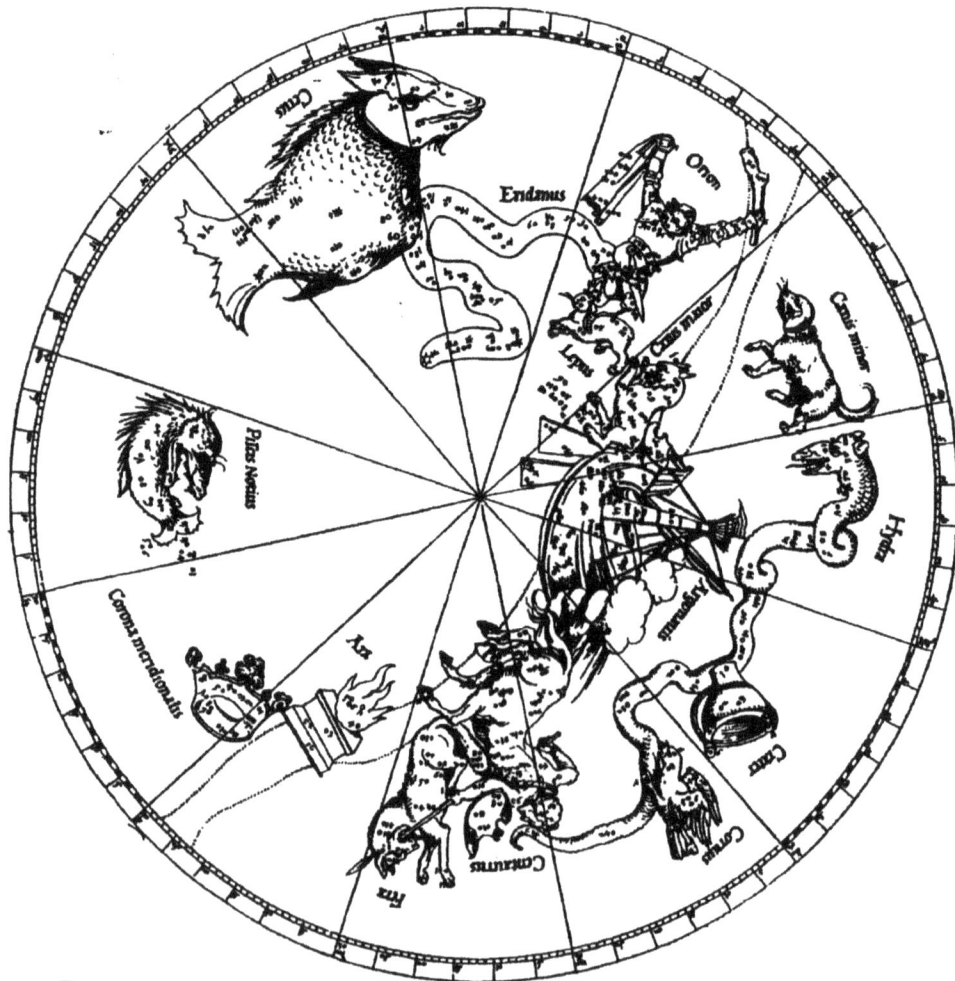

10 INTRODUCING OLIVIA

In this chapter, I would like to introduce the reader to my daughter Olivia. She is an advanced person, reincarnated again to help bring a greater awareness to humankind in the New Age. This section will give you the benefit of her wisdom, and her work for the Hierarchy of Light, which she has already begun, at eight years of age.

A short time after she began talking, Olivia spoke of her adventures in the higher dimensions, before returning here. One day after finishing my daily

trance meditation, I discovered Olivia in my study, sitting in a full Lotus Posture in meditation (She was only two years old at the time). My wife Gayra told me that Olivia got into the room, and that she would have quietly took her out, except that she observed that Olivia quietly sat in meditation with me, and remained so for about an hour. This unusual display of behavior prompted me to begin her esoteric training from that time on. She has been helping me in different ways all along, but a few months before this writing, Olivia began her public work with our study group in Philadelphia. On the first Sunday in June, 1986 she gave her first talk before a group of people.

Olivia has, as her mentors from the Hierarchy, the ascended masters Kwan Yin, Kuthumi, and Jesus the Christ. On numerous occaisions she has demonstrated the truth of this to others, as well as myself.

In the field of Holy Magickal Rites and Spells, her ability has been demonstrated in the preparation of Mystic Oils for various purposes. We will share these with the readers of this work at this time. But first I must admonish the reader to take this seriously; remember the blessed words in the Holy Bible, "whoever enters the Kingdom of God must first become as a child." Again, "a little child shall lead them."

What follows in this chapter is the revelation
that Olivia wishes to share with you.

Dear friend, I am happy to meet you through my
father's book. The oil formulas that I want to share
with you now, were channelled through me from the
higher world. Blessed oils do work because oil stands
for the Holy Spirit. In the Bible, the prophets would
touch people with olive oil. Sometimes they would mix
flowers and herbs in the oils. and these different oils
were used for different reasons. Please don't doubt
any formula, because if you do you will hold yourself
back from getting results. Have faith in God and in
these wonderful things that he made. Mystical things
are important, and you must not play with them. You
must do these things with your whole heart.

#1. HELPING OIL
Mix some Myrhh, Hyssop and Temple Incense in some olive
oil. This is for helping yourself to do what you need
to do.

Put a little of this between your eyebrows, on your
wrists, and on the soles of your feet every morning.
Then pray for a helping hand to accomplish what you
have to do that day.

#2. MONEY OIL

Mix one crushed Bayleaf, some Five Finger Grass, and Frankincense in some oil. Pray that you will have money for whatever you need, while you pour a little on the palms of your hands. Don't worry-have peace and faith, and do this during your quiet time every night.

#3. PROTECTION OIL

Mix some Uncrossing Incense, Frankincense, and Sandalwood Incense into some olive oil.

Place some on both your thumbs, your heels, and on the back of your neck where your energy is stored, every morning. Pray to your special watcher for extra protection that day. Also pray to your watcher every night to make sure nothing hurts you while you are sleeping.

#4. LOVE AND FRIENDSHIP OIL

Mix some Love Attraction Incense, Hyssop and one crushed Bayleaf in olive oil.

Place some on both sides of the neck, the wrists and close to the heart. Do this every day. Pray for more love and friendship to come into your life.

Now, I must tell you some things about life, that is on my heart.

SELFISHNESS AND SHARING

Consider selfishness; do you know someone who is selfish towards you or others? Have you even noticed this trait in yourself? this is one thing we should get rid of.

I knew someone who was selfish. If she held something, she would say it was hers, even if it belonged to someone else. I knew that to act like this is of a low vibration, and I did not care to be around such a person. But I prayed for her, and she is doing much better now.

We must always know that what we hold on to in a selfish way is not ours anyway. Only when we share will we have anything. Remember this.

If you are selfish, you are mostly by yourself. but if you learn to share, you will always have friends.

CLOUDS AND STARS

STARS ARE THERE BY DAY, CLOUDS ARE THERE BY NIGHT. BUT WE CANNOT SEE EITHER AT THE TIMES I SAID BECAUSE OF THE STRANGE WAYS OF LIGHT. THINK ABOUT THIS-THINGS DO NOT ALWAYS APPEAR BECAUSE THEY ARE THERE, THINGS ARE NOT ALWAYS WHAT THEY SEEM..

Love and Light,
Olivia

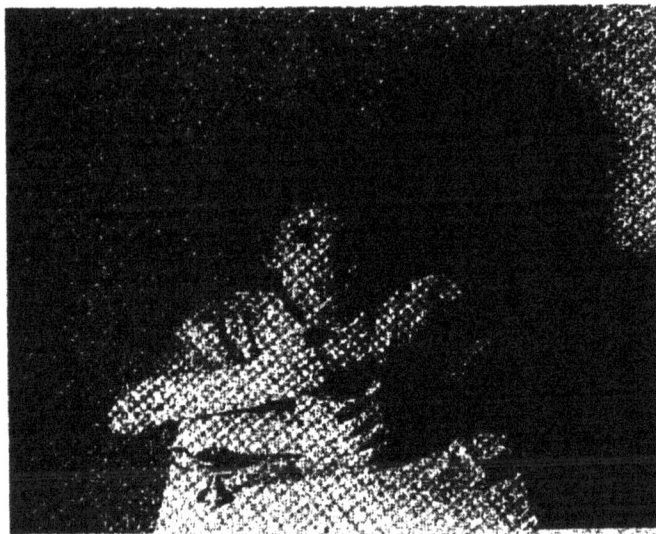

OLIVIA

PERFORMING

HER

WORK

11 MAGICAL DIAGRAMS AND ILLUSTRATIONS

Many esoteric ideas and moods can be inspired by illustration and art. In this chapter I would like to share a few of these immortal illustrations that reveal inner truth.

The diagram below is one of Rosicrucian Origin. It reveals the building of King Solomon's Temple, or the reshaping of our lives at all levels (note the Rose Cross at the top of the illustration).

Mystic adepts have always known that music can have a spell-like effect on people and animals. In the Holy Bible we find reference to this in the story of how David was able to sooth the troubled soul of King Saul with music. During the middle ages, such stories as "the Pied Piper of Hamlet" illustrated this fact.

Illustrations and tales about a knight or warrior slay-
ing a dragon, is symbolic of the triumph of good over
evil. All of us must, sooner or later, face the false
self and destroy it, so that the true self may shine.

Good and evil gods have been described in different
ways by the ancients. God was usually illustrated as
an old man with a long beard, seated on a throne. The
devil was described as an ugly half man—half monster
with a tail and horns. In some cases throughout history,
these descriptions were reversed. In the illustrations
below, the God Odin appears at the right. To the left
is the devil as the seven headed beast in the Book of
Revelation.

In all nations and ages, there have been wise ones
who penetrated into and understood life's mysteries.
Some of these unusual people lived in seclusion, and
few of this class wrote down or discussed their great
wisdom. But there were some who gave audience to others
who sought after this wisdom. They formed mystery
schools, wrote books and performed miracles. Many
people from all walks of life came to the wise to be
helped in many ways.

At their time of departing this physical life, the
wise ones imparted their most secret magickal wisdom
to one or a few of their most advanced disciples.
In this manner were many of the great secret spells
and workings of nature preserved. At this time of
greater awareness, the world is ready to receive such
knowledge more openly.

The American Indians were advanced in the magick of
spells and herbal potions. they observed many things
about life, and thereby attained to great wisdom of
the inner workings of nature.

All creation is governed by law. The principles that operate in the outer universe, discoverable by scientists, are called natural laws. But there are subtler laws that rule the hidden spiritual planes and the inner realm of consciousness. Contained within these laws (or conditions) is the true nature of matter. Knowledge of these laws has an effect upon the mental urges. Mind is the builder. Stay in full mindfulness of the application of Universal Law as related to self and to others, and know that in love all life is given, in love all things move.

In giving one attains. In giving one acquires. In giving, love becomes the fulfilment of desire, guided and directed in the ways that bring the more perfect knowledge of self as related to the universal, all powerful, all guiding, all divine influence in life. Love IS life. When we go back, merge with the God Source, in some infinitesimal but profound way, we expand the Mind of God.

Our God and higher self always points the best and most perfect way and it is ours to listen and choose or reject what we hear. God does not blame, but patiently tries again to show the perfect way, the loving way. All of creation pushes forth. We are ever becoming. Identity ever remains!

1. The Law of Abundance. (sometimes referred to as the Law of Opulence or Success.)

By creating visualizations of abundance in our lives we draw this energy of success into our reality. Success or abundance does not only apply to money. There is success in communication, spirituality, relationships and so on. When creating the abundance of financial gain remember to be IN this world, but not OF this world. We are not the sum total of your possessions.

2. The Law of Action.

No matter what we feel or know, no matter what our potential gifts or talents, only action brings them to life. Those of us who think we understand concepts, such as commitment, courage, and love, one day discover that we only create knowingness when we act; doing becomes understanding. Every aspirant is a focal point of energy and should be a conscious focal point. In the midst of the

whirl and storm (of the chaos of third dimension) s/he should make his/her presence felt.

3. The Law of Akasha.

A great cosmic law which is the principle of the intelligence of substance.

4. The Law of Analogy.

Although this is a definite condition of third dimension existence, no analogy is ever exact in detail but only in certain broad basic correspondences. There will be found unchangeable points of resemblance, but in using analogy viewing creation, no two details are exact. Using analogy in trying to mentally explain the unexplainable, one attempts to convey understanding, in a broad sense.

5. The Law of Ascension.

This law defines the high vibrational frequency which the soul of an incarnational being is resonating. When a personality looses the illusion of separation from it's god self, the vibration of that person raises to the point of ascension. No longer does this mean that the incarnational personality leaves the earth plane to live a finer existence. We are meant to bring our loving energies to our every day existence, becoming an example or role model for others to emulate. We can recognize this vibrational frequency in others by the degree to which they are a magnet to others.

6. The Law of Attraction.

This is the basic law of all manifestation, the Love Aspect, and it governs the Soul aspect. One of the Three Major Laws, and it has 11 subsidiary laws. Fundamentally, this law describes the compelling force of attraction that holds our solar system to the Sirian. It holds our planets revolving around our central unit, the sun. It holds the lesser systems of atomic and molecular matter circulating around a center in the planet, and that of the subtle bodies co-ordinated

around their microcosmic center. It is the primary law of man. The law of synthesis is beginning to be felt.

7. The Law of Balance or Equipoise. (fair exchange)

This is elaboration and continuation of the law of equalities. The law of balance is a universal law that supersedes all of man's laws, creating stability for all third dimension manifestation. Each thought must be balanced by whomever creates it. This is divine wisdom. Allow all viewpoints without feeling you must defend your own. Allow no one to tell you what your journey must reflect or what your reality is. Do not give your power away so easily, but give your love unconditionally. Any messages communicated in love validates equality. Low self esteem is just as non productive as a puffed up sense of self esteem. They both deny equality. Another manifestation of the imbalance of this law is addiction.

8. The Law of Challenge.

We have the right to ask of another his or her intent, identity, and whatever pertinent information we feel we require when encountering a disembodied being. Those who come to us in the roll of information givers to channelers don't mind being challenged. Ask the entity your questions three times (using the same words each time) and you will be given the correct information.

9. The Law of Chemical Affinity.

This law governs the soul aspect in the mineral kingdom. It concerns the marriage of the atoms, and the romance of the elements. It serves to perpetuate the life of the mineral kingdom and to preserve its integrity. It is the cause of the immetalisation of the Monad.

10. The Law of Cohesion.

One of the seven laws of our solar system, under the three major laws. On the second plane cohesion is first apparent. It is the first molecular plane of the system, and is the home of the Monad. Divine coherency is demonstrated.

11. The Law of Color.

All colors are centers of attraction, and are complementary or are antipathetic to each other. Color is healing and impacts the physical, emotional, mental and human body profoundly. Man is partially composed of color in the aura (we are color, tone, symbols and speed of vibration, or light). When intense rays of one or more colors are sent to a specific area of the body, change results.

12. The Law of Common Ground.

This is viewed as a problem solving approach and is an area where two or more can gather to blend differences. It demands that the area be cleansed of previous energy left by others who historically have passed through, or lived on the spot. This is done by two or more sending loving energy to the area for a specified period of time. Cage the area with a gold net and it will stay cleansed of other's energy. You will leave your energy, but that can be cleansed once you have used this space and are leaving.

13. The Law of Consciousness.

As consciousness expands, the space for events increases and therefore the dimensions in which man congizes good and evil, opportunity and possibilities, past-present-future enlarge to reveal the outstanding needs in this present world cycle.

14. The Law of Continuity of Consciousness.

The Universe is in a continuous and endless process of creation. Cosmic consciousness is a reality, and everything in creation is connected to everything else. The medium for the 'implicate order' of this relationship is consciousness. The fusion of individual consciousness and the universal consciousness (the building of the antahkarana) results in the development of universal knowledge, of omniscience (all science/all knowledge). Continuity of consciousness is achieved by us after the soul has been acknowledged, awakened, liberated and identified with the Whole (enlightenment). A step to achieve enlightenment is to be aware of our thoughts, emotions and actions, the faculty that enables us to be vigilant, observant or to know.

15. The Law of Cycles.

The world of nature exists within a larger pattern of cycles, such as day and night and the passing of the seasons. The seasons do not push one another. Neither do clouds race the wind across the sky. All things happen in good time. Everything as a time to rise, and a time to fall. Whatever rises, falls and whatever falls shall rise again. That is the principle of cycles.

16. The Law of Cyclic Return.

Otherwise known as the wheel of reincarnation, once a soul qualifies for an incarnation to third dimension, there is an understanding that it must be completed. Reincarnation is that process by which the 'consciousness of the permanent atom' manifests in another body through the human birthing process. (This accounts for the fact of genius in the very young.) All karma must be cleared or forgiven and certain aspects of soul growth accomplished before this entire episode of reincarnational growth is considered finished .

17. The Law or Right to Decree. (Divine Invocation)

This particular law exists for those working in service to others. Self serving beings will find this law ineffective. This law allows the ascended realms to move from the confines of the Law of Non-Intervention to act on our behalf. Add the phrase to your decree, "Under the Law of Grace" as this is an 'out' clause which will not allow us to manifest or invoke anything which would be detrimental to our existence or not of the highest interest for all, and remain karmic free. In order for your decree to work it must be invoked three times. An Example - "By Divine Decree, in the name of (Yahweh, God, Jesus, Ascend Masters, healing Angels, Mother Mary, My I AM self, etc.) and under the Law of Grace, I ask for _____. It is done, and I thank you." Say the entire request three times, then let it go - trust it is in higher hands.

18. The Law of Discipline.

By practicing discipline, one expands the entity to a greater degree than almost any other action. Discipline is the surest means to

greater freedom and independence. It provides the focus to achieve the skill level and depth of knowledge that translates into more options in life. Commitment involves discipline over a specific period of time. Discipline and commitment provide the bridge between here and our goals.

19. The Law of Disintegration.

One of the seven laws of our solar system, under the three major laws. On the third plane comes the final casting-off, the ultimate shedding of the sheaths, of the fivefold superman. A Chohan of the sixth Initiation discards all the sheaths beneath the monadic vehicle, from the atmic to the physical.

20. The Law of Divine Flow.

By living in the moment, centering ourselves in love and being in service to others (as opposed to service to self), we live in the law of divine flow. We stay in the moment by moment flowing of our higher self, creating actions which reflect love and allowingness. When we are able to do this, we notice how we say just the right things, do what is best for all, and refrain from doing that which we previously disliked in ourselves or others. We maintain a stronger connection to our God self. The more we do this, the more we are able to do this. To a degree, the deliberate letting go of this flow is the allowing of our spiritual integrity to be compromised.

21. The Law of Divine Love and Oneness.

This Law concerns the ability of an entity to complete a round of reincarnation, develop such soul growth that the vibrational speed of the being qualifies him/her to merge with God. We then become a soul extension of God and among our choices many we have the ability to live in the liquid light which flows in and from God, or reincarnate as an avatar in third dimensional existence with the purpose of aiding mankind.

22. The Law of Economy.

The Brahma aspect of the Logos is characterized by that method in the wide distribution of matter, the scattering of the atoms of matter and their dissociation from one another, vibratory rhythm, heterogeneity and quality and their inherent rotary action. This Law of Economy causes matter always to follow the line of least resistance, and is the basis of the separative action of atomic matter. It governs matter, the opposite pole of spirit. Initiates must master this law before they can achieve liberation, or enlightenment.

23. The Law of Economy of Force.

One of the three major laws. The Activity Aspect. This is the law which adjusts all that concerns the material and spiritual evolution of the cosmos to the best possible advantage and with the least expenditure of force. It is the law of the physical atom, and makes perfect each atom of time and each eternal period and carries all onward and upward and through, with the least possible effort with the proper adjustment of equilibrium and with the necessary rate of rate of rhythm. Unevenness of rhythm is really an illusion of time, and does not exist in the cosmic center. We need to ponder on this, for it holds the secret of peace, and we need to grasp the significance of that word through, for it describes the next racial expansion of consciousness, and has a hidden meaning. The person who aims at providing a point of contact between conditions of chaos and Those Who work for constructive ends and order, should likewise use that most necessary factor of common-sense in all that s/he does. This involves always obedience to the law of economy of force, due to discrimination, and a true sense of values. Where these are present, time will be economized, energy will be wisely distributed, excessive zeal will be eliminated, and the Great Ones will be able to depend upon an aspirant's sagacity and thus find a helper.

24. The Law of Equalities (or Analogy),

otherwise known as the Principle of Correspondence or Essential Divinity. "As above, so below; as below, so above." The major linking agent in the universe is the energy of love-wisdom, and the purpose of analogy is to lead the mind back toward the sense of oneness (enlightenment). The thoughts and images we hold in our conscious and subconscious minds will manifest their mirror likenesses in our external circumstances. Our outer world is a

mirror of our inner world. Earth is a school for practicing these laws of mind control. There is a Correspondence between the Laws and Phenomena of the various planes of Being and Life. This principle enables the phenomenon of Discernment, Intuition, Hunches, etc. and that which is called remote viewing or out of body experience. Correspondence enables that which is normally unknowable, to become known to the individual who learns and knows how to use this principle. Some use it in a conscious and deliberate manner while others may not even be aware that they are using this principle. When used knowingly, it will enhance the clarity of vision and enables the mind to penetrate the most secret of secrets, and can shed light on many a dark paradox. Correspondence establishes the interconnectedness between all things in the universe and keeps all things relative to each other. Known to the adepts and masters of ancient Egypt as the substance of the ethereal, the spirit substance or web that pervades and interpenetrates the universe. This substance acts as a medium for the transmission of light, heat, electricity, gravity. It is non-material in nature. Also known as the un-created substance, or universal substance. The substance in which all suns, worlds, and galaxies are suspended in space, time, and change. All of us are intimately connected to all of the above mentioned events, and to each other, whether or not it is realized. The ethers are where spirit substance is manifesting the beginning of matter. Science refers to this substance as "dark matter" that cannot be seen, touched, smelled, or weighed. Dark matter does not absorb or reflect light and is therefore invisible. It is considered to be a non material substance. It was first discovered on Earth while doing research with the Hubble space telescope. The planes of Correspondence in the order of manifestation are, The Great Spiritual Plane; The Great Mental Plane; The Great Physical Plane, or the Trinity (the ascending scale of life and being).

25. The Law of Expansion.

This law of a gradual evolutionary expansion of the consciousness indwelling every form is the cause of the spheroidal form of every life in the entire solar system. It is a fact in nature that all that is in existence dwells within a sphere. The sphere requires two types of force - rotary and spiral-cyclic to produce its own internal activity. The law of relativity, or the relation between all atoms, which produces that which is called Light, and which in its aggregated phenomena, forms that composite sphere, a solar

system. It is also known as the law of expansive response, and its symbol is the flaming rosy sun with a sign in the center, a sign symbolizing the union of fire and water. . The ray energy is expansive energy of the 3rd ray, the adapting factor.

26. The Law of Expectation.

Energy follows thought; we move toward but not beyond what we can imagine. What we assume, expect or believe colors and creates our experience. By changing our expectations, we change our experience of every aspect of life.

27. The Law of Faith.

The Law of Faith is founded upon the recognition that we know more than we have read, heard, or studied. We Know more because we Are a part of the ALL. We have a direct link to universal wisdom. We only have to look within, listen, discern, then trust. We need to develop more trust in our own deepest intuition and wisdom as the final arbiter and source of our decisions.

28. The Law of Fixation.

One of the seven laws of our solar system, under the three major laws, and governs the time of an individual's rebirth. This is the governing law on the mental plane, finding its greater correspondence in the Law of Karma on cosmic mental levels, and has a close connection with manas, the fifth principle. 'As a man thinks, so is he,' according to his thoughts are his desires and acts, and so results the future. The mind controls and stabilizes, and coherency is the result.

29. The Law of Flexibility.

This law involves a pragmatic acceptance of the present moment. We accept ourselves, others and current circumstances rather than a rigid resistance of the moment. It requires an alert and expansive state of awareness, and embracing and making constructive use of the moment. Stumbling blocks become stepping stones and problems become opportunities. Everything serves our highest good

if we make good use of it. The serenity prayer used by Alcoholics Anonymous and other twelve step programs reflects this law. "God grant me the serenity to accept the things I cannot change, the courage to change the things I can, and the wisdom to know the difference." This prayer was drawn from Buddha's writings.

30. The Law of Forgiveness.

This law works with the energy of allowingness, and seeing all as love, so one may dispense with the unnatural feeling of getting even. The old energy of an eye for an eye keeps the vibrations of a person very low. To forgive, to release old anger, allows the law of grace to intercede and dispense with amounts of karma an individual has stored in his or her akasha. Non-violence is the natural outgrowth of the law of forgiveness and love. All good comes from forgiveness. It is a truth that the continuation of the human species is due to man's being forgiving. Forgiveness is holiness. By forgiveness the universe is held together. Forgiveness is the might of the mighty; forgiveness is quiet of mind. Forgiveness and gentleness are the qualities of the self-possessed, and represent eternal virtue.

31. The Law of Free Will, or the Law of Choice.

We in third dimension have the right to expand or contract, to bring our creative and expressive energies out into the world in positive or negative ways. This is our ultimate decision. Not all of existence lives with this law as it carries with it both the possibility of great soul growth and the ability to loose soul growth and create evil or negativity. No matter what our circumstances, we have the power to choose our direction. We also choose to be under the influence of others or choose to be an example for others. We do it with a hundred actions which lead to the circumstances we find ourselves in today. Thoughts are things and the mind is the builder. The free will we use to create mixes with our ability to love profoundly, and therefore this path reflects the duration of the time spent in attempt to merge with the Great Soul of all Creation. The Christ warned of that which could destroy the soul (not Spirit) so there is always a possibility that a soul entity on its journey could become a God-hater with diminished light and be absorbed back into the Spirit of God to become just spirit and no longer a soul with separate awareness. A goal of our higher selves is to

voluntarily and willingly surrender our egos to be a perfected spirit, hanging up the Soul-Overcoat of manifestation regardless of how many lifetimes it takes.

32. The Law of Gender.

This law embodies the Truth that gender is manifested in everything - the masculine and feminine law is ever at work on all planes of causation. Gender manifests on all three planes of causation which are the great spiritual plane, the great mental plane, and the great physical plane. The law is always the same on all planes, but on the higher planes, it takes higher forms of manifestation. This law works in the direction of generation, regeneration, and creation. All life forms contain the two elements of gender - masculine and feminine. On the great physical plane, the sexes of all species are manifested as male and female and the role they play in sexual reproduction. On the great mental plane, gender manifests as masculine and feminine energies that exist within each and every person. Every male has its female element, and every female has its male element. On the great spiritual plane, gender manifests as the Father-Mother principle of the Infinite Omnipresent God in whose mind the universe is conceived and firmly held. It is written, "We all live, move, and have our being within God. When balance and learning reach a critical mass, the personality achieves the merger of God, and see self as neither male or female, but as one blended self.

33. The Law of Good Will.

Knowledge of this law will help those who have feelings of futility when thinking about the course of world events. By viewing life in terms of energy, we understand that our higher self coupled with our thought/mind action creates, and our actions/energy solidifies this thought into matter or results. In an energy relationship there is always a positive, creating side and a negative, receiving side of that creative relation. This is simply how the world works. The will-to-good is the positive, creative impetus, which, when received, makes the manifestation of goodwill possible. We are either mentally polarized or emotionally polarized, and only those who are mentally polarized can begin to appropriate this energy through will on the mental plane. When this is fully comprehended, we begin to realize why the manifestation of goodwill is not more widespread.

Djwhal Khul states that "It is absolutely essential that the will-to-good be unfolded by the disciples of the world, so that goodwill can be expressed by the rank and file of mankind. The will-to-good of the world knowers is the magnetic seed of the future." From *Rays and the Initiations*. p. 110. Our mental capacity today readily contacts those ideas which constitute the purpose behind the form. We have the ability to mentally construct a happening, and see it through to completion. This is will-to-good. The desire of one to create a loving scenario is 'goodwill', another but related action. The will-to-good is always an education process where the recipients are left free to receive the idea or not. The responsibility for expanding the amount of goodwill in the world directly lays on the shoulders of the intelligentsia of the world. In the goodwill process it is the creative/idea/problem solving individuals who are directly responsible for creating goodwill. The "rank and file" of humanity simply do not yet possess the mental capability to evoke the process yet, even though many are able to participate in the process. This knowledge should fill the responsible group with a greater amount of hope and assurance, because they have the power to generate goodwill in their every day routine solving of problems. Djwhal Khul says in *Esoteric Healing*, p. 545, "When the majority of the inhabitants of the earth are being rapidly oriented towards good, towards righteousness, as the Bible expresses it, and when the bulk of human beings are inclined towards goodwill 'then ill health will persistently, even if only gradually, disappear and die out and finally become nonexistent. Slowly, very slowly this is already happening'"

34. The Law of Grace.

This can waive the Law of Karma. When applied, this law allows a person to receive more than one deserves or works for if it is in the highest good for all. When called upon, this law allows the person to send another a healing, to do soul talk, use divine decree, etc. and not suffer the consequences of karma incurrence, or interfere with the receiver's soul plan. The wording to insert in the request is "Under the Law of Grace." Another aspect of this law is to be of higher vibration to consistently live in grace. i.e. A loving person who works diligently sending world healing to Mother Earth and all on her body, and focusing so much on this activity, while shopping she forgets her car meter has expired. In all

probability her car will not receive a ticket for this expiration. This condition can not be abused or it will leave.

35. The Law of Group Endeavor.

This law defines the multiplying of energy one creates when acting with like minded individuals to form a group effort to pray, manifest, do lightwork, or even to create degrees of control which we define as evil or black magic. Where the efforts of an individual may equal one unit, the efforts of two praying or healing for a common goal with equal energy will effect the energy of twenty units instead of the sum total of two. With three, the resultant energy explodes further. The longer pure thought (the exclusion of any other thought) of one's desired goal is held in the mind, the more powerful the result. Holding a pure thought for an increment of time is the beginning lesson of manifestation.

36. The Law of Group Life.

Not only must man fulfill in love his family and national obligations, but he must think in the wider terms of humanity itself, and so bring the Law of Brotherhood into _expression. Brotherhood is a group quality. Questions of self such as "Will my action tend to the group good? Will the group suffer or hurt if I do this action?" Abiding by these actions will gradually become part of our racial consciousness, and our civilization will adjust itself to these new conditions. All aspects of life of God are interdependent, and when one proceeds to fuller _expression, all of the group benefit.

37. The Law of Group Progress.

This law is also known as the law of elevation. The symbol is the mountain and the goat standing at the summit with the astrological sign of Capricorn. (All hard places can be surmounted and the summit reached by the Divine Goat - a symbol meaning group effort.) The ray energy is progressive energy of the 7th ray, the evolving factor.

38. The Law of Healing.

This law concerns the ability of one to channel energy (prana - chi - holy spirit) which radiates from the Source we call God. The

purpose of this channeled energy is to either improve self or another by removing blockages or instilling the sacred energy which pulsates from the Source of God. With intent or technique we may send this energy to the past, present, or future. Hands-on healers who are effective in healing have brain waves at 7.8 Hz - the same as the earth's pulse beat. Their brain waves are in sync with the earth's at the time the healing is performed. Another aspect of this law is the ability of one in third dimension to heal self by that which triggers a leap in faith.

39. The Law of Higher Will.

From the viewpoint of our separate self and smaller will, it's normal to act on the basis of our own desires and preferences. When we surrender our smaller self and will to the guidance of a higher will and dedicate our actions for the highest good of ALL concerned, we feel an inspired glow at the center of our life.

40. The Law of Honesty.

Recognizing, accepting and expressing our authentic interior reality lies at the heart of honesty. Only when we are honest with ourselves can we speak or act honestly with anyone else. In the sense of integrity, honesty entails acting in line with higher laws despite negative impulses to the contrary. We don't need to be punished for breaking spiritual law or higher laws. The act itself is the punishment and sets into motion subtle forces whose natural consequences we cannot escape any more than we are able to escape the force of gravity. When we let fear stop us from expressing our true feelings and needs, we are being dishonest with ourselves and it costs us a sense of energy and spirit.

41. The Law of Identity.

This law pertains to the individual right of all to create one's own beingness. It applies to the time spent between incarnations as well as third dimension incarnational experiences. When an entity merges with the Great Central Sun/God, the entity still may separate to accomplish something, and will possess his/her individual identity.

42. The Law of Intention.

When a person's intention is held in the mind and action of the physical effort does not follow, people create false impressions of self. He or she thinks self is good or better than actions prove. Energy must follow intention for that which is perceived as good to happen. When an act of kindness is performed and intention is such that one wishes to be recognized for goodness, or has underlying motivation which is not of the higher order, higher rewards will not be forthcoming. Intention and effort must be of the higher vibration to gain or create spiritual accomplishment and reward. If a person gives a promise to another to do something and has an intention to do so, but does not follow through with action, this becomes a lie, a breaking of one's word, and creates karma.

43. The Law of Intuition.

We can only get in touch with our own source of intuition and wisdom when we no longer depend upon others' opinions for our sense of identity or worth. Do we value and trust our own intuition, or do we value and transfer authority to the opinions of others over our own inner feelings? Our intuition becomes more profound when we claim our own sacred identity.

44. The Law of Inverse Proportions. (Longevity)

One need not die if the pranic life force is not lost but increased, and drawn from the Cosmic source, conquering death and fate. The span of life is related to the rate of breathing. If the span of life is 120 years and the normal person breathed 21,600 times per day, that is 15 respirations per minute. If the rate of breathing is 18 per minute, however, the span of life will be about 96 years. If because of poor living habits and needless expenditure of energy the average rate of breathing is 30 per minute, the life span will be only 60 years. If the rate is slowed through yogic practices and self control to an average of only 5 respirations per minute the life span will be 360 years. If it is one per minute, the life span will increase to 1,800 years. If the rate of breathing is reduced to zero, the life span becomes infinity. The secret of longevity lies in the technique of diverting the breathing to the subtle channels and centers.

45. The Law of Justice.

This law upholds creation's farthest swinging orb. The functioning of this law is instantaneous for people of God-realization. They have banished forever all thwarting crosscurrents of ego. The universe conspires for retribution.

46. The Law of Karma.

This is the natural principle of cause and effect. Every cause has its' effect; every effect has its cause. Everything happens according to law. Chance is but a name for law not recognized. There are many planes of causation, but nothing escapes the law. It is ever at work with chains of causations and effects that govern all of life and manifested matter. If a person was to follow each chain link of causation, it will be found that it has its beginning and endings in the non material realm, the realm of spirit. It affects the throwing of dice on a gambling table or a rock slide that is caused by rain and wind. Each can be followed and understood to the observing mind which sees the cycles in all things, and realizes that all things follow the Great Law. The law itself is illusive and cannot be proven other than observed with the mind and is used to determine the causations and effects of any event. When this law is used with conscious effort, desired results can be produced in a person's life by steering him or herself along definite paths of causation. When the law is used in an unconscious and haphazard mind, the effects could become potentially disastrous for the individual or group of individuals. So called "accidents" could occur without warning to individuals who toil through life without awareness. We are responsible for the very thoughts that we produce and the final result of our own mental alchemy. Fear is one of the most dangerous mental causation that prevents a person from thinking and acting as the higher self would prefer. The cause of fear is the result of a lack of knowledge about the unknown God which should be the most important educational journey in a person's life. The causation of fear can only be removed through knowledge, wisdom, and understanding Universal Law, the reality that we live in order to produce the desired effects in our lives. The greatest evil under the sun according to Hermes/Thoth, is Not knowing God. In every minute thought, action, and deed that is performed, a person sets into motion unseen chains of causations and effects which will vibrate from the mental plane throughout the entire cellular structure of body, out into the environment, and finally into the

cosmos. Eventually the vibratory energy returns to its originator upon the return swing of the pendulum. All this in less time than the twinkling of an eye. Because there are seven dimensions of reality in which causations can occur, we remain unaware of many reasons for effects. By understanding Universal laws we can learn to operate in grace instead of accumulating karma (restrictive). This law is mechanically or mathematically operative; its workings may be scientifically manipulated by men and women of divine wisdom (fully realized). The karmic law requires that every human wish find ultimate fulfilment. Therefore, desire is the chain that binds man to the reincarnational wheel. Karma is attracted only where the magnet of the personal ego still exists. An understanding of karma as the law of justice underlying life's inequalities serves to free the human mind from resentment against God and man.

47. The Law of Knowledge.

This law concerns the fact that all knowledge concerns energy, its application, and its use or misuse. Much information is withheld from a person until s/he is a disciple, and still more until he is a pledged initiate. Information is not as necessary to the training of the disciple or initiate as is the proper use of thought energy. (i.e. Full Mindfulness) Knowledge is the right apprehension of the laws of energy, of the conservation of force, of the sources of energy, of its qualities, its types and its vibrations.

48. The Law of the Lotus.

This refers to the egoic lotus or the 'Flowering of Self' and includes knowledge, love and sacrifice.

49. The Law of Love.

One of the seven laws of our solar system, under the three major laws. This is the law of the astral plane. It aims at the transmutation of the desire nature (love in the personality), and links it up with the greater magentism of the love aspect on the buddhic plane (love in the Triad), and the Monads of Love. These three points mark periods of completion, and starting points for fresh endeavor in the life of the evolving Monad - from the personality to the

Triad, from the Triad to the Monad, from the Monad back again to its Source. Love limits itself by desire.

50. The Law of the Lower Four.

This law is also known as the law of etheric union, and its symbol is a male and female form, placed back to back. The male figure is holding above his head a shield or tray of silver, a great reflector, while the female form holds aloft an urn full of oil. Below this sign is another hieroglyphic which contains the secret of the astral plane, which has to be dominated by the mental. The ray energy is fiery energy of the 5th ray, the vitalizing factor.

51. The Law of Magnetic Control.

One of the seven laws of our solar system, under the three major laws. This holds paramount on the buddhic plane, and in the development of the control of this law, lies hid the control of the personality by the Monad via the egoic body. A second description on a very physical/man level, is that every thought we have creates a match that comes back to us like a boomerang.

52. The Law of Magnetic Impulse.

Also known as the first step towards marriage, or the law of the polar union. It results in an eventual union between the man or atom and the group which produces harmonious group relations. It is also known as the law of the polar union, and the symbol is two fiery balls united by a triangle of fire, thus picturing the triple interplay between all atomic structures. The ray energy is radiatory energy of the 2nd ray. Manifesting factor.

53. The Law of Magnetism.

This is the law which produces the unifying of a personality, and though it is an _expression of lunar force, is of a higher order than the law of physical sex. The three aspects are the stage of high intellectuality, or of artistic attainment. Second is the stage of discipleship. Third is the stage of treading the Path.

54. The Law of Manifestation.

There are actions, sounds, techniques, mental energy and symbols which when understood, will enable one to manifest first energy (love, more joy, peace, etc.) into one's aura, then with practice and increased love held in the heart and emotional body - physical objects. Thought is a force, even as electricity or gravitation. The human mind is a spark of the almighty consciousness of God. Whatever the powerful mind (holding a pure thought - that which excludes any other thought) believes very intensely will instantly come to pass.

55. The Law of Mantras.

Each mantra is a linkage to a certain aspect of the absolute, a certain manifestation of Divinity. In true mantra practice, one forgets the fact that the self is chanting, becomes the mantra itself, and attains the state where nothing but the mantra exists. One's being then connects with the higher being the mantra represents if it is the name of a Master Being, or connects with the ray of light emanating from God if it is a sound (aum or om, hu, etc.). The practice of chanting mantras is profoundly beneficial in raising the vibration of self.

56. The Law of Meditation.

This law is defined as a current of unified thought. It is a continuum of mental effort to assimilate the object of meditation, free from any other effort to assimilate other objects. The very least that may happen is the calming of self. When meditating on God, the most profound happening will bring a merging of the two, or enlightenment, as Buddhists call this occurrence.

57. The Law of Mentalism.

"THE ALL IS MIND" The All is substantial reality underlying all the outward manifestations and appearances which we know as empirical. The material universe, phenomena, matter, energy and all that is apparent to our material senses. It is spirit indefinable, unknowable, and thought of as a universal, infinite, living mind. This Law explains the true nature of energy, power and matter. The

Universe is mental in nature, and mental transmutation is the art of changing the conditions of the universe, along the lines of matter, force, and mind. The atom of matter, the unit of force, the mind of man, and the being of the arch-angel are all but degrees in one scale, and all fundamentally the same. The difference is solely a matter of degree and rate of vibration. All are creations of the All, and have their existence solely within the Infinite Mind of the All.

58. The Law of Miracles.

This law is operable by any person who has realized that the essence of creation is light. A master is able to employ his/her divine knowledge of light phenomena to project instantly into perceptible manifestation the ubiquitous light atoms. The actual form of the projection (whatever it is, water into wine, medicine, a human body) is determined by the master's wish and by his/her powers of will and visualization. All events in our precisely adjusted universe are lawfully wrought and lawfully explicable. The so-called miraculous powers of a great master are a natural accompaniment to his/her exact understanding of subtle laws that operate in the inner cosmos of consciousness. Nothing is a miracle except in the profound sense that everything is a miracle. Is anything more miraculous than that each of us is encased in an intricately organized body, and is set upon on earth whirling through space among the stars?

59. The Law of Monadic Return.

This law concerns the 'force of evolution' and is the sum total of three influences. The strength of vibrations from the seven stars of the Great Bear depend upon the closeness of the connection and the accuracy of the alignment between any particular Heavenly Man and His Prototype. Second is the Seven Sisters, or the Pleiades. Third is the sun Sirius. It is the appearance or the disappearance of these waves of life-force which sweeps into incarnation the divine pilgrims, and which brings about the cyclic manifestation of such great Lives as the 'Silent Watcher' and the 'Great Sacrifice.' Within limits, man is the controller of his destiny, wielding forces and energies, manipulating lesser lives and controlling lesser centers of energy, and as time passes, his radius of control becomes eve more extensive.

60. The Law of No Judgements.

The Universal Spirit does not judge us; judgements are human inventions, a means to compare, contrast and control as we judge ourselves against artificial, and often idealistic standards of perfection, morality or truth. Under the law of equalities, our judgements attract judgement to us in equal measure. The life/karmic review conducted by yourself after death is a condition of living in duality/third dimension.

61. The Law of Non-Attachment.

Attachment to the self creates karma. Non-attachment to the self dissolves karma. This non-attachment to the self is made possible through the realization that the ultimate nature of the self is Empty. The self does not exist as a separate entity. A full conceptual understanding needs to occur, but mere conceptual understanding does not lead to liberation. Many methods have been devised to help human beings attain this realization, and usually fall into two categories. The first is 'non-attached behavior' and the other is called 'spiritual practice.' Through diligent application of these methods, an individual can free him or herself from the confines of karmically determined existence. Enlightenment is real and attainable.

62. The Law of Non-Intervention.

This law concerns the individual rights of people and society situations to serve self rather than live in the vibration of service to others. This law prevents physical beings and non physical beings from intervening or correcting what they see as wrong or harmful. If this law is violated, there is great karma incurring. Another aspect of this law is that spirit is not permitted to channel material to a recipient that would force a change in the evolution of the person. There is an exception when the channeler is willing to undergo a trance, and the consciousness leaves the body for another consciousness to enter and impart knowledge that was previously unknown to the individual.

63. The Law of One.

The Lord is ONE. All that is, is His - of self, of the universe, of the activities in the earth. All moves and has its being in Him. So it is in self. Life itself is the consciousness, the awareness of that Oneness of that Universal Consciousness in the earth.

64. The Law of Order of Creation.

The beginning of law carries all the way through. And that which comes or begins first is conceived in spirit, grows in the mental and manifests in the material. First it was the means and source or manner by which the powers that be made the centralization for making known to the children of men, and children of God, the directing forces or powers. Man eventually turned this into that channel for destructive forces. While man developed in this direction for many centuries, humans are leaning toward light. We are reaching toward the critical point of more in the light than in darkness.

65. The Law of Patience.

Luke said – "In your patience possess ye your souls." Patience involves spiritual, mental and physical thought and action. Through it, we learn to know our self, to measure and test our ideals, to use faith and to seek understanding through all the other virtues. Patience allows all other virtues to manifest more profoundly. Patiently we realize that any fault we see in another is one we have personal knowledge of from prior experience. Patiently we seek true understanding, not just knowledge, as we realize that every soul is totally unique and will come to its enlightenment in its own time.

66. The Law of Patterns.

Any habit or pattern, whether we call it good or bad, tends to reassert itself over time unless we break that pattern by doing something different. If it is good, we can reinforce the pattern with small self-rewards. We have the power of spontaneous action, doing old things in new ways, changing and restructuring our lives and our behavior. Some of our change ability is dictated by the ways we learned when we were young. We learned to make sense of the world by observing patterns, and this has survival value. We

can correct the patterns we see as dysfunctional, negative or destructive by doing something different that will have sufficient impact to interrupt the old pattern.

67. The Law of Perfection.

This law concerns the absolute perfection of the process of our unfolding. From a transcendental perspective, everyone and everything is unconditionally perfect. From a conventional viewpoint, perfection doesn't exist. Excellence is the best we can achieve, and achieving it takes time and practice. When we understand the larger picture, we understand our role and responsibility in helping the world we live in to become more loving, giving, kinder and gentler. When we live up to this responsibility, we expand into the perfection of our higher selves.

68. The Law of Periodicity.

Training for the aspirant will by cyclic, and will have its ebb and flow, as all else in nature. Times of activity succeed times of pralaya, and periods of registered contact alternate with periods of apparent silence. If the student develops as desired, each pralayic period is succeeded by one of greater activity, and of more potent achievement. Rhythm, ebb and flow, and the measured beat of the pulsating life are ever the law of the universe. In learning to respond to the vibration of the high Places, this rhythmic periodicity must be borne in mind.

69. The Law of Planetary Affinity.

This law is concerned with the connection of the interaction of the planets with each other and their eventual marriage.

70. The Law of Polarity.

Everything is Dual. Everything has poles. Everything has its pair of opposites. Like and unlike are the same. Opposites are identical in nature, but different in degree. All paradoxes may be reconciled. The evidence of this principle is observed in the polarity of planets and the various celestial bodies that includes our earth, solar

system, and galaxy. Everything has polarity. Without the law of polarity - light, gravity and electricity would not be possible. On the mental plane, this principle manifests itself in the heart center of each person as the enlightened or dark mind. The Principle of Polarity makes possible the choices we make on the scale of life between good and evil, right and wrong, generosity and greed, love and fear, truth and lies. The law of cause and effect is closely connected to polarity and holds us true to the choices and actions we make by returning to us what we have measured out to others. Like the swing of the pendulum, it always returns where it began. In biblical terms it is expressed as, "Whatsoever a man sows, so shall he reap." "Do unto others, as you would have them to you." This principle establishes the paradox or the dual aspects of reality. "Everything that is, has its double." Positive and negative, light and darkness, hot and cold, Love and fear, mortality and Immortality.

71. The Law of Prayer and Meditation.

Prayer is a conscious concerted effort to commune with the Consciousness of Life and its Creator and thus we speak to God. Prayer is also an aligning, cleansing process opening up our inner-selves to the Source of all life and demonstrating that we are anxious for enlightenment and guidance. In prayer we speak to God but so often we do not wait for a reply. Meditation is the freeing and emptying of ourselves of obstacles that hinder communication and allow us to channel the God-Force, spiritually, mentally and physically. Meditation is likened to God speaking to us, and is the attunement of our physical and mental bodies to their spiritual Source. "Be still and know that I am God." In meditation, correctly aligned and unobstructed, the Creative Forces of God can rise along spiritual and physical channels in our bodies and be disseminated through sensitive spiritual chakras. Prayer is the precursor of meditation. Meditate regularly as we meet the Living God within the temple of our own body, cleansed and consecrated.

72. The Law of the Present Moment.

Time does not exist. What we refer to as past and future, have no reality except in our own mental constructs. The idea of time is a convention of thought and language, a social agreement. In truth, we only have this moment. When we hold regret for an occurrence in the past we keep the regret alive with pictures and feelings we

conjure up. When we feel anxiety about the future, we keep the anxiety alive with the pictures we imagine. Time is the abstract concept. When we practice remembering that the here and now is all we have, our present moments improve.

73. The Law of Process.

This law is an awareness that we have things to accomplish in our life. If we wish to reach a certain goal, we must set a direction (create order), prepare well and proceed in small but sure steps. Any achievement can be managed in increments. Skipping a single step or taking a shortcut often results in failure. Also included in this law is the knowing to appreciate the accomplishment of a step toward a goal.

74. The Law of Progress.
It is the basis of the phenomenon of sensation, which is the key to this solar system of love, our system being a 'Son of Necessity' or desire. This law is the working out into manifestation of the informing consciousness of a part of the deva kingdom, and of certain pranic energies.

75. The Law of Prophecy.

The only true future that exists is the desire or will of the Source of all Creation that none shall be lost and that the future is happening, unfolding in the I AM, now. Sacred geometry is an aspect, a manifestation of God's love. People who are able to tune into the Akashic records and into the Universal Consciousness are sometimes using sacred geometry to draw a line from the supposed past, present and then to the future. The ability to use sacred geometry comes with the raising of vibration to such a degree, the personality gains the right to assess Akasha for the good of another or self. When reading the energy going to the future of people on earth one must keep in mind that this energy changes from moment to moment. While those powerful prophets of old were correct in their time and some of what they said has held to present day, much of their prophecies have lost relevancy. Just by hearing prediction, we change the outcome to some degree.

76. The Law of Radiation.

This _expression of Divine Activity is one of the most practical utility. Understanding radiatory, or emanatory condition of all substances as a specific point in evolution allows one to approach Reality. It is the outer effect produced by all forms in all kingdoms when their internal activity has reached such a stage of vibratory activity that the confining walls of the form no longer form a prison, but permit the liberation of the subjective essence. Liberation means the ability of any conscious atom to pass out of one sphere of energized influence into another of a higher vibration of a larger and wider expanse of conscious realization.

77. The Law of Rebirth.

Each life is an assuming of ancient obligations, a recovery of old relations, an opportunity for the paying of old indebtedness, a chance to make restitution and progress, an awakening of deep-seated qualities, a recognition of old friends and enemies, the solution of revolting injustices and the explanation of that which conditions the man and makes him what he is. This law, when understood, will do much to solve the problems of sex and marriage. It will create a person who treads more carefully on the path of life.

78. The Law of Rebound.

The law of rebound concerns the right of one to come out of a negative situation stronger and bolder and with more soul growth than previously experienced. This has been used as an example in stories since the beginning of mankind. Traumatic situations create the need for rebound, and the soul often seeks these negative occurrences to give self and observers a leap in faith.

79. The Law of Repulse.

This is also known as the law of all destroying angels, and its symbol is an angel with a flaming sword, turning in all directions. It is the Angel guarding the treasure, driving man forth in search of anothe way of entrance, thus forcing him through the cycle of

rebirth until he finds the portal of initiation. The ray energy is rejecting energy of lst ray, the dispersing factor.

80. The Law of Responsibility.

It was God's idea to separate, to give our soul existence. It was our idea to go away from God into materiality with the original purpose of profound and speedy soul growth. There are some souls who have experienced, to some degree, soul loss. God is responsible for us through love and we are responsible to become or reclaim this divine love. Once we establish the limits and boundaries of our responsibility, we can take full charge of that which is our duty and let go of that which is not. We find more enjoyment supporting others as we create more harmonious co-operative relationships by understanding that which falls within our realm of responsibility. Under this law we understand a person's need to over co-operate to such an extent that one becomes co-dependent - the condition which is obsessive focus on other people's lives. This law reminds us to respect our internal values and find our own point of balance.

81. The Law of Rhythm.

Everything flows, out and in; everything has its' tides; all things rise and fall; the pendulum-swing manifests in everything; the measure of the swing to the right is the measure of the swing to the left; rhythm compensates. This principle, on the Physical Plane, is the most visible of all principles and its power is observed within the forces of nature which move the waves and tides of our oceans and the continuous changes of the seasons. It is observed in the continuous cycles of life, death, and the rebirth of all things, a rise and fall of governments and nations, a constant creation and destruction of suns, worlds, and galaxies. On the plane of energy it is observed in the behavior of the alternating current wave of electricity, light, and heat as it vibrates between the positive and negative pole. Rhythm on the mental plane is experienced as the wide mood swings displayed in human nature. It can be experienced as extreme happiness, and then swing to extreme sadness - from a gentle behavior to an extremely violent behavior at the blink of an eye. Rhythm is the law of compensation and maintains the equilibrium in all things. It returns to us what we measure out in life. The return swing of the pendulum is assured without fail and there is no escape from the effects of this

92

immutable law. This law holds us true to what we believe, or not believe, and compensates us accordingly. All of nature follows this law. Rhythm perpetuates the phenomenon of time. The pendulum-like swing of rhythm is immutable and we can only counteract its backward swing by mentally polarizing ourselves in a desirable position on the scale of life. It requires a dedicated personal commitment to cultivate the unknown within all of us in order to cause a quantum leap in the evolutionary process of life with all its aches and pains. This is a mental art that is known to hierophants, adepts, and masters of all ages. We will fulfil the law one way or another. Either use the law to our advantage, or become its subject. The door of universal law swings in all directions. The final result depends what we have chosen to believe and whether or not our belief system allows us to see the truth as it really is. If we do not want to know or do not care, then we will evolve through the standard process of evolution. Nothing can, or is allowed to stand still. All manifestation is the result of active energy producing certain results, and expenditure of energy in any one direction will necessitate an equal expenditure in an opposite direction.

82. The Law of Right Human Relations.

This law helps us define limits of behavioral control with others in third dimension. Let no one assume to forcibly teach, counsel or guide, for we all have the greatest of these we could hope for already within us. While each teacher is in a manner a director, the individual person may only be a means - not - a way of life. A strong action may promote refusal and achieve rejection, or it may encourage one to become dependent on another's will. By not searching for excellence within, one refuses the gifts already there but not recognized or realized. In our relationships we achieve greater results with others by our own fine example and also listening. People answer their own questions if given enough opportunity. The only real control we ever have and need is with self.

83. The Law of Right to One's Own Space.

This is an aspect of free will, but another law of its own. Everyone is entitled to make career decisions for self, decide the belief system one feels comfortable with, and generally create the life that will allow one to fulfil his or her own birth vision. This is the right

to one's own space, the right to live one's own life (allowing for parental direction in the developing young person). Overprotective or controlling parents, friends and even dictators have impeded this law and right since almost the inception of mankind.

84. The Law of Sacrifice (and Death).

One of the seven laws of our solar system, under the three major laws. This is the controlling factor on the physical plane. The destruction of the form, in order that the evolving life may progress, is one of the fundamental methods in evolution. This is crucifixion, the basic law of all group work, the governing principle which results in each human unit eventually becoming a Savior. It is also known as the Law of those who choose to die. The symbol is a rosy cross with a golden bird hovering above it. The ray energy is out-pouring 4th ray. At-one-ing factor.

85. The Law of Schools. (The Law of Love and Light.)

This is a mysterious term used to cover the law as it affects the expansions of consciousness which an initiate undergoes, and his ability to attract to himself through knowledge, 1 - his own Higher Self, so as to produce alignment and illumination, 2 - his Guru, 3 - that which he seeks to know, 4 - that which he can utilize in his work of service, 5 - other souls with whom he can work. This law applies to the initiate who has transcended the stage of self-consciousness.

86. The Law of Service.

The law or science of service grows naturally out of the successful application of the sciences of the antahkarana and meditation, and is the governing law of the future. With the linking of soul and personality the light of the soul pours into the brain consciousness, resulting in the subordination of the lower to the higher. This identification produces a corresponding activity in the personal life and the activity we call service. Therein lies the growth through the service of the race, and through a cultivated self-forgetfulness. Service is the true science of creation and is a scientific method of establishing continuity. This is also known as the law of water and of fishes. The symbol is a pitcher on the head of a man who

stands in the form of a cross. This law is the governing factor of the age of Aquarius. The ray energy is out-going energy of the 6th ray, vivifying factor. If the evasion of this law is a conscious action, there are karmic penalties. This work requires so much sacrifice of time and personal interest, requiring deliberate effort, conscious wisdom and the ability to work without attachment.

87. The Law of Sex.

This is the term applied to the force which brings about the physical merging of the two poles in connection with the animal kingdom, and of man, viewing him as responsive to the call of his/her animal nature. It concerns itself with the due guarding of the form in this particular cycle and its perpetuation. It is only powerful during the period of the duality of the sexes and their separation and, in the case of man, will be offset by a higher _expression of the law when man is again androgynous.

88. The Law of Solar Evolution.

This law is the sum total of all the lesser activities.

89. The Law of Solar Union.

When the interplay of the Suns is being dealt with from the material aspect and from the consciousness aspect, this term is occultly used. It is not possible to enlarge upon it.

90. The Law of Sound.

Every living thing in existence has a sound. Through this knowledge changes will be brought about and new forms developed through its medium. The release of energy in the atom is linked to the science of sound. Healing with sound is profoundly effective (vocal sounds - tuning forks - music). Sound has the power to restore people to their harmonic patterns. Chanting specific sounds and mantrams brings about great healing and raising of vibration, and produces virtually unimaginable results when done with group mantric chanting. The most powerful mantram known to present man is 'Om mani padme hum'.

91. The Law of Spiritual Approach.

This law depicts the conscious act of a personality to create with its every thought, word and deed the ability to be the reflection of its god self. Every action is a prayer to the Creator of All. When this is done with success, the personality becomes a mirror or reflection of the god self for others to learn from and emulate. This is a walking, talking example of becoming our higher self.

92. The Law of Spiritual Awakening.

A basic level of self-control and stability is required to maintain the degree of effort required for the awakening of other states of awareness. Because such awakening brings with it higher forms of perception and power, self-centered misuse of the greater perception and power bears proportionally graver karmic consequence. Spiritual Awakening brings with it the need for moral impeccability.

93. The Law of Summons.

Otherwise known as soul talk, one can learn how to lift the soul from the physical body and summon another soul, to have a soul to soul talk. This is most powerful because there is no conscious ego present. The message of love and or explanation, or plea is received in a most profound manner.

94. The Law of Surrender.

Because people so cherish the self, surrendering is a very frightening experience. A person may experience the surrender as a leap into an abyss or as death. This may be perceived because s/he has not yet attained a complete trust and faith in God, the complete assurance that once the self is abandoned, the being automatically merges with a higher stage of existence which is necessarily ready and waiting to accept it. There is no chance for the process not to function. At the instant of surrender, the entire being of the individual merges into the specific higher manifestation of reality that it is in relation to at that point in its development. God streams into the soul that has managed to negate the self. This is the surrender of the idea of I.

95. The Law of Synthesis.

The Will aspect. One of the three major laws. Although this law is almost impossible for any but the buddhic faculty to understand the scope of this law, it demonstrates the fact that all things - abstract and concrete - exist as one. It is a unit of His thought, a thought form in its entirety, a concrete whole, and not the differentiated process that we feel our evolving system to be. It is the sum total, the center and the periphery, and the circle of manifestation regarded as a unit. It is the primary law of a Heavenly Man. The law of attraction has full sway. The law of economy is transcended.

96. The Law of Teaching.

This law concerns the responsibility people have to pass on that which they learn, for the continuation of the human race to benefit by this information, if it is in the higher interest of people to learn the acquired information.

97. The Law of Telepathy.

The will, projected from the point between the eyebrows, is known as the broadcasting apparatus of thought. When the feeling is calmly concentrated on the heart, it acts as a mental radio, and can receive the messages of others from far or near. In telepathy the fine vibrations of thoughts in one person's mind are transmitted through the subtle vibrations of astral ether and then through the grosser earthly ether, creating electrical waves which, in turn, translate themselves into thought waves in the mind of another person.

98. The Law of Three Requests.

Whenever we pray or request a higher power to assist, we bring stronger energy to the effort by repeating our request/prayer three times.

99. The Law of Time.

The only moment we have is now. This is where we create. What

we have done is done and that moment in history exists only as a record or energy trace in time and space. The consequences of past actions are atoned through karma, and can be rewritten to a degree. The FUTURE only ever happens in and from the present tense and is built of today's thoughts, dressed by emotion and driven by action. Activity is the key. Third dimension living has more rigid structure of time than fourth dimension existence. There are those who can slip into 'no time' but these are people who have raised their personal vibration (demonstrating many virtues, dispensed a great deal of karma and much killing of the ego) and accessed the information to create the ability. Third dimension linear time was created for those living under this veil of forgetfulness to center in the moment and perceive a sense of order without the remembrance of burdens of past lives.

100. The Law of Unconditional Love.

This is a condition as well as a law of third dimension living. Loving ourselves and other people as they are, is honoring self and another's self and soul path. It is loving without judgement or reservation, an awareness we are all part of God or the All. When we love without condition or restraint we connect in a profound manner with our own higher self. We notice that we say the right things at the right time in our communication with others while loving unconditionally. Life and events seem to flow to us in a more joyous and agreeable manner. Everything seems easy when living in unconditional love.

101. The Law of Unity.

We are all connected, all bearing the seed of Divinity. This is the way we start, and the way we develop into eternity. It is only while in third dimension physical form, and because of the greater separation of our higher self from the personality, we experience the illusion that we stand alone. Fear enters our emotional body because of this illusion and begins to close more profoundly our connection to the Source. Also, when we experience great soul growth, in some small but profound manner, all benefit. All substance in this Universe flows to us and through us. We are All.

102. The Law of Universal Sympathy.

This law concerns a yogic power which allows a Yogi (a person who is devoid of the ego-principle) to transfer information, or influence others' minds.

103. The Law of Vibration.

One of the seven laws of our solar system, under the three major laws. This is the basis of manifestation, starting on the first plane, the beginning of the work of the Logos. This is the atomic law of the system, in the same sense that on each of our planes the first subplane is the atomic plane. Nothing rests; everything moves; everything vibrates. This is the law of progress, of movement and of rotation. This Principle explains that the differences between manifestations of matter, energy, mind and spirit, result largely from varying rates in vibration. All that exists, is in constant vibration and motion. Atoms always vibrate with such great rapidity that they seem motionless to the physical eye. At the other end of the scale are things that vibrate so slowly that they also appear to be motionless or non-existent. In between are the various vibrations of living entities which range from consciousness all the way down to the lowly dust particle that plays an important role in the food chain. Still there are things even lower then dust. If we were to follow the scale of life all the way down to the utmost regions of the negative pole (undifferentiated matter), we again would find ourselves in the realm of spirit - the Alpha, and the Omega. All that is, begins in spirit and ends in spirit completing a single cycle of evolution that will be repeated countless numbers of times through eternity.

104. The Law of Will of God.

The creators of our world carry out their work of form-building under this law. God's working has to do with things free from change and movement - things divine. It is God's will that what is human should be divine, and therefore all creation pushes forth to the God Light. God is all good, and it is by reason of the Good that all other things exist.

105. The Law of Will Power.

This law concerns the individual drive within a soul

extension/personality which is projected from the complete entity. The individual developing soul extension differs in degree of will power from its other entity extensions/soul family members. Depending on the conditions of an incarnational experience and the incoming will of this extension, the personality can possess a drive to accomplish something that may seem overwhelming to others in the soul family and/or other incarnational personalities (friends). This law depicts the right and condition of each personality or soul extension to generate it's own degree of will power.

THE MYSTICAL DIMENSIONS OF THE UNIVERSE

In order to better understand **Godspells**, one must have a better understanding of the complexities of the Universe. According to the ancient book of hidden knowledge, **The Kybalion**, here is a harmony, agreement, and correspondence between the several planes of Manifestation, Life and Being. This truth is a truth because all that is included in the Universe emanates from the same source, and the same laws, principles, and characteristics apply to each unit, or combination of units of activity, as each manifests its own phenomena upon its own plane.

The Universe may be divided into three great classes of phenomena, known as the Three Great Planes, namely:

I. The Great Physical Plane.

II. The Great Mental Plane.

III. The Great Spiritual Plane.

These divisions are more or less artificial and arbitrary, for the truth is that all of the three divisions are but ascending degrees of the great scale of Life, the lowest point of which is undifferentiated Matter, and the highest point that of Spirit. And, moreover, the different Planes shade into each other, so that no hard and fast division may be made between the higher phenomena of the Physical and the lower of the Mental; or between the higher of the Mental and the lower of the Physical.

In short, the Three Great Planes may be regarded as three great groups of degrees of Life Manifestation. At the beginning we may as well consider the question so often asked by the neophyte, who desires to be informed regarding the meaning of the word "Plane," which term has been very freely used, and very poorly explained,

in many recent works upon the subject of occultism, The question is generally about as fellows: "Is a Plane a place having dimensions, or is it merely a condition or state?" We answer: "No, not a place, nor ordinary dimension of space; and yet more than a state or condition. it may be considered as a state or condition, and yet the state or condition is a degree of dimension, in a scale subject to measurement."

Somewhat paradoxical, is it not? But let us examine the matter. A "dimension," you know, is "a measure in a straight line, relating to measure," etc. The ordinary dimensions of space are length, breadth, and height, or perhaps length, breadth, height, thickness or circumference. But there is another dimension of "created things," or "measure in a straight line," known to occultists, and to scientists as well, although the latter have not as yet applied the term "dimension" to it–and this new dimension, which, by the way, is the much speculated about "Fourth Dimension," is the standard used in determining the degrees or "planes."

This Fourth Dimension may be called "the Dimension of Vibration." It is a fact well known to modern science that "everything is in motion; everything vibrates; nothing is at rest."

From the highest manifestation, to the lowest, everything and all things Vibrate. Not only do they vibrate at different rates of motion, but as in different directions and in a different manner. The degrees of the "rate" of vibrations constitute the degrees of measurement on the Scale of Vibrations–in other words the degrees of the Fourth Dimension. The higher the degree of rate of vibration, the higher the plane, and the higher the manifestation of Life occupying that plane. So that while a plane is not "a place," nor yet "a state or condition," yet it possesses qualities common to both.

You will kindly remember, however, that the Three Great Planes are not actual divisions of the phenomena of the Universe, but merely arbitrary terms used by the ancients in order to aid in the thought and study of the various degrees and forms of universal activity and life. The atom of matter, the unit of force, the mind of man, and the being of the archangel are all but degrees in one scale, and all fundamentally the same, the difference between solely a matter of degree, and rate of vibration–all are creations of THE ALL, and have their existence solely within the Infinite Mind of THE ALL.

The ancients sub-divide each of the Three Great Planes into Seven Minor Planes, and each of these latter are also sub-divided into

seven sub-planes, all divisions being more or less arbitrary, shading into each other, and adopted merely for convenience of scientific study and thought.

The Great Physical Plane, and its Seven Minor Planes, is that division of the phenomena of the Universe which includes all that relates to physics, or material things, forces, and manifestations. It includes all forms of that which we call Matter, and all forms of that which we call Energy or Force. But you must remember that Magikal Philosophy does not recognize Matter as a "thing in itself," or as having a separate existence even in the Mind of THE ALL. The Teachings are that Matter is but a form of Energy–that is, Energy at a low rate of vibrations of a certain kind. And accordingly the ancient masters classify Matter under the head of Energy, and give to it three of the Seven Minor Planes of the Great Physical Plane.

These Seven Minor Physical Planes are as follows:

I. The Plane of Matter (A).

II. The Plane of Matter (B).

III. The Plane of Matter (C).

IV. The Plane of Ethereal Substance.

V. The Plane of Energy (A).

VI. The Plane of Energy (B).

VII. The Plane of Energy (C).

The Plane of Matter (A) comprises the forms of Matter in its form of solids, liquids, and gases, as generally recognized by the text-books on physics. The Plane of Matter (B) comprises certain higher and more subtle forms of Matter of the existence of which modern science is but now recognizing, the phenomena of Radiant Matter, in its phases of radium, etc., belonging to the lower sub-division of this Minor Plane. The Plane of Matter (C) comprises forms of the most subtle and tenuous Matter, the existence of which is not suspected by ordinary scientists. The Plane of Ethereal Substance comprises that which science speaks of as "The Ether," a substance of extreme tenuity and elasticity, pervading all Universal Space, and acting as a medium for the transmission of waves of energy, such as light, heat, electricity, etc. This Ethereal Substance forms a connecting link between

Matter (so-called) and Energy, and partakes of the nature of each. The ancient Masters, however, instruct that this plane has seven

sub-divisions (as have all of the Minor Planes), and that in fact there are seven ethers, instead of but one.

Next above the Plane of Ethereal Substance comes the Plane of Energy (A), which comprises the ordinary forms of Energy known to science, its seven sub-planes being, respectively, Heat; Light; Magnetism; Electricity, and Attraction (including Gravitation, Cohesion, Chemical Affinity, etc.) and several other forms of energy indicated by scientific experiments but not as yet named or classified. The Plane of Energy (B) comprises seven sub-planes of higher forms of energy not as yet discovered by science, but which have been called "Nature's Finer Forces" and which are called into operation in manifestations of certain forms of mental phenomena, and by which such phenomena becomes possible. The Plane of Energy (C) comprises seven sub-planes of energy so highly organized that it bears many of the characteristics of "life," but which is not recognized by the minds of men on the ordinary plane of development, being available for the use on beings of the Spiritual Plane alone–such energy is unthinkable to ordinary man, and may be considered almost as "the divine power." The beings employing the same are as "gods" compared even to the highest human types known to us.

The Great Mental Plane comprises those forms of "living things" known to us in ordinary life, as well as certain other forms not so well known except to the occultist. The classification of the Seven Minor Mental Planes is more or less satisfactory and arbitrary (unless accompanied by elaborate explanations which are foreign to the purpose of this particular work), but we may as well mention them. They are as follows:

I. The Plane of Mineral Mind.

II. The Plane of Elemental Mind (A).

III. The Plane of Plant Mind.

IV. The Plane of Elemental Mind (B)

V. The Plane of Animal Mind.

VI. The Plane of Elemental Mind (C).

VII. The Plane of Human Mind.

The Plane of Mineral Mind comprises the "states or conditions" of the units or entities, or groups and combinations of the same, which animate the forms known to us as "minerals, chemicals, etc." These entities must not be confounded with the molecules, atoms and

corpuscles themselves, the latter being merely the material bodies or forms of these entities, just as a man's body is but his material form and not "himself." These entities may be called "souls "in one sense, and are living beings of a low degree of development, life, and mind– just a little more than the units of "living energy" which comprise the higher sub-divisions of the highest Physical Plane. The average mind does not generally attribute the possession of mind, soul, or life, to the Mineral kingdom, but all occultists recognize the existence of the same, and modern science is rapidly moving forward to the point-of-view of the Hermetic, in this respect. The molecules, atoms and corpuscles have their "loves and hates"; likes and dislikes; "attractions and repulsions"; "affinities and non-affinities," etc., and some of the more daring of modern scientific minds have expressed the opinion that the desire and will, emotions and feelings, of the atoms differ only in degree from those of men. We have no time or space to argue this matter here. All occultists know it to be a fact, and others are referred to some of the more recent scientific works for outside corroboration. There are the usual seven sub-divisions to this plane.

The Plane of Elemental Mind (A) comprises the state or condition, and degree of mental and vital development of a class of entities unknown to the average man, but recognized to occultists. They are invisible to the ordinary senses of man, but, nevertheless, exist and play their part of the Drama of the Universe. Their degree of intelligence is between that of the mineral and chemical entities on the one hand, and of the entities of the plant kingdom on the other. There are seven sub-divisions to this plane, also.

The Plane of Plant Mind, in its seven sub-divisions, comprises the states or conditions of the entities comprising the kingdoms of the Plant World, the vital and mental phenomena of which is fairly well understood by the average intelligent person, many new and interesting scientific works regarding "Mind and Life in Plants" having been published during the last decade. Plants have life, mind and "souls," as well as have the animals, man, and superman.

The Plane of Elemental Mind (B), in its seven sub-divisions, comprises the states and conditions of a higher form of "elemental" or unseen entities, playing their part in the general work of the Universe, the mind and life of which form a part of the scale between the Plane of Plant Mind and the Plane of Animal Mind, the entities partaking of the nature of both.

The Plane of Animal Mind, in its seven sub-divisions, comprises the states and conditions of the entities, beings, or souls, animating the

animal forms of life, familiar to us all. It is not necessary to go into details regarding this kingdom or plane of life, for the animal world is as familiar to us as is our own.

The Plane of Elemental Mind (C), in its seven sub-divisions, comprises those entities or beings, invisible as are all such elemental forms, which partake of the nature of both animal and human life in a degree and in certain combinations. The highest forms are semi-human in intelligence.

The Plane of Human Mind, in its seven sub-divisions, comprises those manifestations of life and mentality which are common to Man, in his various grades, degrees, and division. In this connection, we wish to point out the fact that the average man of today occupies but the fourth sub-division of the Plane of Human Mind, and only the most intelligent have crossed the borders of the Fifth Sub-Division. It has taken the race millions of years to reach this stage, and it will take many more years for the race to move on to the sixth and seventh subdivisions, and beyond. But, remember, that there have been races before us which have passed through these degrees, and then on to higher planes. Our own race is the fifth (with stragglers from the fourth) which has set foot upon The Path. And, then there are a few advanced souls of our own race who have outstripped the masses, and who have passed on to the sixth and seventh sub-division, and some few being still further on. The man of the Sixth Sub-Division will be "The Super-Man"; he of the Seventh will be "The Over-Man."

In our consideration of the Seven Minor Mental Planes, we have merely referred to the Three Elementary Planes in a general way. We do not wish to go into this subject in detail in this work, for it does not belong to this part of the general philosophy and teachings. But we may say this much, in order to give you a little clearer idea of the relations of these planes to the more familiar ones–the Elementary Planes bear the same relation to the Planes of Mineral, Plant, Animal and Human Mentality and Life, that the black keys on the piano do to the white keys. The white keys are sufficient to produce music, but there are certain scales, melodies, and harmonies, in which the black keys play their part, and in which their presence is necessary. They are also necessary as "connecting links" of soul-condition; entity states, etc., between the several other planes, certain forms of development being attained therein– this last fact giving to the reader who can "read between the lines" a new light upon the processes of Evolution, and a new key to the secret door of the "leaps of life" between kingdom and

kingdom. The great kingdoms of Elementals are fully recognized by all occultists, and the esoteric writings are full of mention of them. The readers of Bulwer's "Zanoni" and similar tales will recognize the entities inhabiting these planes of life.

Passing on from the Great Mental Plane to the Great Spiritual Plane, what shall we say? How can we explain these higher states of Being, Life and Mind, to minds as yet unable to grasp and understand the higher sub-divisions of the Plane of Human Mind? The task is impossible. We can speak only in the most general terms. How may Light be described to a man born blind–how sugar, to a man who has never tasted anything sweet–how harmony, to one born deaf?

All that we can say is that the Seven Minor Planes of the Great Spiritual Plane (each Minor Plane having its seven sub-divisions) comprise Beings possessing Life, Mind and Form as far above that of Man of to-day as the latter is above the earthworm, mineral or even certain forms of Energy or Matter. The Life of these Beings so far transcends ours, that we cannot even think of the details of the same; their Minds so far transcend ours, that to them we scarcely seem to "think," and our mental processes seem almost akin to material processes; the Matter of which their forms are composed is of the highest Planes of Matter, nay, some are even said to be "clothed in Pure Energy." What may be said of such Beings?

On the Seven Minor Planes of the Great Spiritual Plane exist Beings of whom we may speak as Angels; Archangels; Demi-Gods. On the lower Minor Planes dwell those great souls whom we call Masters and Adepts. Above them come the Great Hierarchies of the

Angelic Hosts, unthinkable to man; and above those come those who may without irreverence be called "The Gods," so high in the scale of Being are they, their being, intelligence and power being akin to those attributed by the races of men to their conceptions of Deity. These Beings are beyond even the highest flights of the human imagination, the word "Divine" being the only one applicable to them. Many of these Beings, as well as the Angelic Host, take the greatest interest in the affairs of the Universe and play an important part in its affairs. These Unseen Divinities and Angelic Helpers extend their influence freely and powerfully, in the process of Evolution, and Cosmic Progress. Their occasional intervention and assistance in human affairs have led to the many legends, beliefs, religions and traditions of the race, past and present. They have super-imposed their knowledge and power upon the world, again and again, all under the Law of THE ALL, of course.

But, yet, even the highest of these advanced Beings exist merely as creations of, and in, the Mind of THE ALL, and are subject to the Cosmic Processes and Universal Laws. They are still Mortal. We may call them "gods" if we like, but still they are but the Elder Brethren of the Race,–the advanced souls who have outstripped their brethren, and who have foregone the ecstasy of Absorption by THE ALL, in order to help the race on its upward journey along The Path. But, they belong to the Universe, and are subject to its conditions–they are mortal–and their plane is below that of Absolute Spirit.

Only the most advanced Ascended Masters are able to grasp the Inner Teachings regarding the state of existence, and the powers manifested on the Spiritual Planes. The phenomenon is so much higher than that of the Mental Planes that a confusion of ideas would surely result from an attempt to describe the same. Only those whose minds have been carefully trained along the lines of the Hermetic Philosophy for years–yes, those who have brought with them from other incarnations the knowledge acquired previously – can comprehend just what is meant by the Teaching regarding these Spiritual Planes. And much of these inner Teachings is held by the Great Masters as being too sacred, important and even dangerous for general public dissemination.

The intelligent student may recognize what we mean by this when we state that the meaning of "Spirit" as used by the Masters is akin to "Living Power"; "Animated Force"; "Inner Essence"; "Essence of Life," etc., which meaning must not be confounded with that usually and commonly employed in connection with the term, i.e., "religious; ecclesiastical; spirituelle; ethereal; holy," etc., etc. To occultists the word "Spirit" is used in the sense of "The Animating Principle," carrying with it the idea of Power, Living Energy, Mystic Force, etc. And occultists know that that which is known to them as "Spiritual Power" may be employed for evil as well as good ends (in accordance with the Principle of Polarity), a fact which has been recognized by the majority of religions in their conceptions of Satan, Beelzebub, the Devil, Lucifer, Fallen Angels, etc. And so the knowledge regarding these Planes has been kept in the Holy of Holies in all Esoteric Fraternities and Occult Orders, in the Secret Chamber of the Temple. However, this may be said here, that those who have attained high spiritual powers and have misused them, have a terrible fate in store for them, and the swing of the pendulum of Rhythm will inevitably swing them back to the furthest extreme of Material existence, from which point they must retrace their steps Spiritward, along the weary rounds of The Path, but

always with the added torture of having always with them a lingering memory of the heights from which they fell owing to their evil actions.

The legends of the Fallen Angels have a basis in actual facts, as all advanced occultists know. The striving for selfish power on the Spiritual Planes inevitably results in the selfish soul losing its spiritual balance and falling back as far as it had previously risen. But to even such a soul, the opportunity of a return is given–and such souls make the return journey, paying the terrible penalty according to the invariable Law.

The Principle of Vibration manifests on all planes, in fact the very differences that go to make the "planes" arise from Vibration, as we have explained. The Principle of Polarity manifests on each plane, the extremes of the Poles being apparently opposite and contradictory. The Principle of Rhythm manifests on each Plane, the movement of the phenomena having its ebb and flow, rise and flow, incoming and outgoing. The Principle of Cause and Effect manifests on each Plane, every Effect having its Cause and every Cause having its effect.

AWAKEN YOUR HIDDEN MAGIC

We all have hidden abilities that for one reason or another, normally do not make themselves apparent under normal day to day conditions. It could be that the technological age that we live in has hypnotized us into forgetting that we have theses amazing powers. Whatever the reasons, there are easy ways to reawaken your latent psychic abilities.

The word psychic comes from the Greek word psyche, which means the human soul. Therefore, the word psychic implies the ability to perceive things independent of the physical senses, from within. For this reason psychic abilities are also termed "The Sixth Sense" or "Extra Sensory Perception".

The ancient prophets, yogis and mystics were psychic to an advanced degree, being direct instruments for the will of God. Be aware that instant methods may not be 100% accurate, and that a student should go on to more advanced techniques which we will discuss later. You, as well as every other person, are psychic. Beyond the five physical senses are higher avenues of perception, by which we can read and send thoughts, project into the future and even tune in to the Cosmic Mind for information concerning anything or anyone. However, this Extra Sensory Perception is

dormant in most human beings, except on rare occasions when a positive impression, termed "hunch", is recognized and acted upon.

WHERE DO PSYCHIC IMPRESSIONS COME FROM?

They come from the minds of other people, such as a good friend or loved one reaching out towards us in some way though separated by many miles. Another example is messages we may receive from spiritual sources, such as the souls of the departed, master teachers, guardian angels, and in cases of advanced students, direct communication with God.

PSYCHIC TOOLS

When a person decides to become active in psychic development they should begin by using various props which I call psychic tools until they advance in sensitivity. The point to remember is that practice makes perfect. I will now reveal some very interesting instant psychic techniques of which some require simple props to help focus your psychic energy and awareness.

THE BIBLE

For many generations people have used the Holy Bible as an instrument through which they could obtain psychic guidance. The formula is that one should become quiet, then read the 50th. Psalm out loud in a soft and reverent tone of voice. Next, the inquirer should close the Bible and repeat a sincere prayer, calling upon the help of good spirit guides and angels to reveal the answer to their question. After the prayer, one should speak their question out loud, then run the thumb over the edge of the pages and open the Bible where they feel directed. The final step is to read the first passage which catches the eye. It is believed that the scriptural passage will shed light of understanding on the problem.

"Thy word is a light unto my path" – Psalms 119:105

SIGNS IN THE SKY

This means to discern the shapes of clouds as a psychic omen. To receive information in this manner you should go to the country or a quiet area of a city park. Lie down on the grass, deeply relax and ask your question aloud. Then you just observe the formations

of the clouds above. Some people believe that one or more shapes may be symbolic of people or things which reveal an acceptable solution to their problem.

MYSTIC INCENSE

The burning of incense has been a great psychic tool for thousands of years in mystic and religious practices all over the world. A psychic method to obtain a simple answer of "yes" or "no" is employed by observing the smoke of the incense. The particulars of this method are as follows: Become relaxed and repeat a prayer, followed by asking a question out loud. Then light some Jasmine incense and observe the smoke: If it remains low and moves to the side it is an indication of "no" or "unlikely". If it ascends upward, it signifies "yes" or a favorable influence. You may obtain better results if you burn powdered Jasmine incense by pouring about a teaspoon of it on a burning charcoal tablet which you can obtain from an occult supply house or specialized store.

After you add the incense to the charcoal, drop a few Poppy Seeds on it. This Poppy Seed addition was favored by mystics of the Near East in ancient times.

WATER AND WAX

This method is performed by having a glass half filled with cool water and a candle in your left hand. Relax and utter a prayer for guidance. Next, light the candle and allow it to burn for a few moments, after which you must tilt it over the glass allowing a few drops of hot wax to drip into the water. Observe the shape which the wax takes after it is in the water. Interpret what the shape means to you and convert your observation into an omen of guidance based on its personal symbolism.

WATER AND OIL

This is a very effective method which begins to open the senses of inner awareness to an advanced degree. You will need three white candles, a glass of water and small amount of Olive Oil. Arrange the items on a table and place a drop or two of Olive Oil on the surface of the water. Have the lights out and the candles lit. Gaze at the oil on the surface of the water for several moments. Just relax and allow your mind to drift as you gaze at the surface. After

awhile you should receive mental impressions and should take note of them and the relationship of their symbolism to the answers you seek. You may even have a vision as you gaze at the surface.

This was a method highly favored by the prophets and apostles of the Bible. However, it is still used in modern times. There are two words which stand out in biblical stories in relation to this practice. They are "Urim" and "Thummim". In modern day private rituals a talisman with the word "Urim" is placed on a table to the left of a person, and signifies the answer "no". A talisman with the word "Thummim" is placed to the right and signifies the answer "yes".

The two talismans should be four or five inches apart. Next, you should write down your question on a slip of paper and fold it a few times so that it is small. Hold the paper in your right hand; Close your eyes as you stand before the table. Repeat, mentally or out loud, the words of Psalms 57:7. "My heart is fixed, oh God, my heart is fixed. I will sing and give praise."

Now, with eyes still closed, toss the paper in the direction of the table top. Open your eyes and observe: If the slip of paper fell on or near the "Urim" talisman it is an indication of no, in answer to your question. If on or near the "Thummim" talisman it is an indication of yes. If the slip falls at a fairly even distance between the two it indicates a 50/50 chance. Should you decide to perform this experiment remember that you must flow with the inner power and allow it to manifest.

ADVANCED TECHNIQUES

The previous methods are popular and used by some advanced students as well as beginners. However, there are advanced techniques which develop our ability to see, hear and feel from within at any time we desire to do so, without the aid of tools. This takes faith, devotion and patience. We will now consider the more advanced techniques.

THE ASTRAL TUBE

We can see, with our mind's eye, things which are beyond our human sense of sight. This has been called clairvoyance which means clear vision. By developing this ability we can operate it at will and see beyond solid walls, perceive what others are doing at a distance, project our vision backward or forward in time to view the past and know the future, see beyond the outer appearance of

things and people, thus knowing their true nature. The underlying principle in this ability is to realize that every material thing has its counterpart in the astral world or fourth dimension. By tuning in to this dimension we overcome the limitation imposed by the physical three dimensional world. This tuning in method is called "The Astral Tube" and I will reveal an exercise to develop this ability. But first I would like to tell you about experiences of people, just like you, and how they overcame obstacles by using the astral tube.

MAN SAVES FAMILY

An advanced student was away from home on business. He was a devoted husband and father of three lovely children. While asleep in his motel room he suddenly awoke and noticed that it was three o'clock in the morning. The problem was that he had a horrible feeling that his family was in danger. He got up, said the prescribed prayer and tuned in to his family using the astral tube.

He saw his wife sleeping soundly in their bedroom, then he shifted to each of the children and they also were asleep. An intuition prompted him to project his vision outside the house, and there he saw a burglar attempting to break in. He quickly phoned his wife alerting her to call the police. She did so and the burglar was arrested within a few minutes. It turned out that this burglar was also a rapist and murderer and had been wanted by the police.

Thanks to the psychic ability of this student, his family was saved from a great danger.

WOMAN DISCOVERS SECRET PLOT

A certain woman was a faithful student of these dynamic laws. She was a widow and had a son and daughter-in-law who lived with her. While on vacation she met a man whom she fell in love with and planned to marry. Within a few weeks after her return from the cruise the man came to visit her in Chicago. He stayed at a hotel as a matter of respect for the woman. However, when he left for his hotel room that evening the lady had an uneasy feeling that something was not quite right.

After a sincere prayer she projected her inner vision to his hotel room and discovered what this man really was. He had a woman staying with him who was apparently his partner in crime. She overheard them plotting that after he marry the woman he would swindle a large amount of money from her, then disappear. This

student not only used clairvoyance, but also clairaudience (clear hearing), and this saved her from losing everything. She quickly called the man and informed him that she knew everything, down to an exact description of the woman in his room. He was so shocked that he admitted it and begged her not to call the police. She never heard from him again.

A STUDENT WHO SAW HEAVEN

A young man, just twelve years of age was advancing on the spiritual path and became adept at using the astral tube. His mother became ill and died when he was still an infant. One day he decided to attempt a projection into the abode of spirits in the astral realm. He was able to communicate with a soul guardian who led him to where his mother was, a beautiful paradise. He visited and talked with his mother and she told him things he did not know before. After his experience he related a message to his father about something which happened before his birth. The father, with tears in his eyes, admitted that what the boy told him was true and testified that this was indeed a proof of life after death.

HOW TO DEVELOP AND USE THE ASTRAL TUBE

Plainly speaking, this method constitutes building an imaginary tube between you and your object of consideration, so that you link up with that object and become able to know the unknown. You accomplish this by shifting your emotional energy and will power into the astral dimension, thus lifting the curtain which separates the seen from the unseen. There is a material way to do this which I will now reveal.

You will need, for the astral tube experiment, a piece of aluminium or steel pipe; However, the cardboard tube from a roll of paper towels would do just as well. You will also need a plain candle. Place the candle on a table and seat yourself at the table. Make sure that the wall and surrounding area near the candle is free from distracting objects.

Light the candle and turn all other lights off. Relax, as you have been instructed, then proceed with the next step. Position the tube about three inches from between your eyes. Think of the spot between your eyebrows as you look through the tube at the candle flame. Do this for up to about fifteen minutes at a time. It is best not to overdo it the first few times, just follow your own inner

guidance as to how long and how often you should do this exercise.

In between sessions, you should try to use the astral tube without the prop. It may be awhile, but at a certain point in your development you should be able to use the astral tube for clairvoyance at will. This exercise is an effective way to awaken your inner awareness for psychic vision until a future time, when you will no longer need any outside help, when the power of your will alone activates your inner abilities.

THE INNER EAR

Clairaudience or inner hearing may be developed along with inner vision so that one may hear as. well as see via the astral tube. Practice hearing low sounds that you would not notice ordinarily. Also, you can use the cardboard tube to develop this ability Tune in to the sound which reminds one of the sound of the ocean.

THE PRESCRIBED PRAYER

Before using the astral tube you should repeat the following prayer with conviction and strong emotion. "In the Mind of God is knowledge of all is and shall be. I was created in God's therefore, my mind may work in harmony Father's Mind. I do and shall know all is and shall be according to the Divine I am that That I am."

BEYOND PSYCHIC POWER – THE GIFTS OF THE HOLY SPIRIT

There is a power which transcends the manifestation of our Psyche or Soul, and this power is to connect and channel wisdom from the all powerful Cosmic Mind. This has been called "The Gifts of The Holy Spirit" by some religious teachers. What we must realize is that because of our education, preconceived ideas and programmed opinions, our own soul may not channel a pure, untainted expression from spirit. We may (and often do) color our impressions with deeply rooted opinions and programmed reactions. For this reason the wise student does not stand still at the stage of psychic development but probes deeper into pure spirit energy.

SPIRIT COMMUNICATION

At this very moment you are surrounded by all types of spirits: good, bad, angels, demons, nature spirits, and others of various types and degrees too numerous to mention. These different spirits are attracted to you according to your mental and emotional condition at any given time. For example, if you were in a very undesirable mood you would attract spirits who are also undesirable.

On the other hand, if you were in an exalted or pleasant mood you would attract helpful, friendly spirits. This is based on a universal law of magnetic attraction which the ancients described in the statement, "Like attracts like". Negative spirits are responsible for implanting destructive thoughts in the minds of humans as well as causing misunderstandings and every type of undesirable condition in life. However, positive or good spirits are responsible for all good that we are inspired to accomplish, as well as every perfect thought of harmony, self-improvement and illumination. The more we grow into a state of harmony with the cosmos the more we attract the attention and help from advanced spirits.

YOU CAN TALK WITH GOD

We live in a religious world in which a large percent of the population attends some type of church or religious group. They regularly hear sermons of the God of miracles and power who called and anointed ordinary people to declare his message and perform miracles. Yet, when a person of our generation claims to have had a vision or be in communication with God, a majority of religious people will reject and persecute such a person. The reason is that some people are religious only in outer expressions of worship and do not believe from the heart in the reality of God.

Others believe that the day of miracles is past, and that God is, in some way, disconnected from his creation. There are even some who go to church for mundane or profitable reasons and actually do not believe in God. Dear friend, I declare to you in all truth and sincerity that the day of miracles is not past, and that you can communicate with God through the gifts of the spirit. You may ask, "How can one talk with God"? My direct answer is simple; I can point the way but you must travel the path. Does every person understand how they move about and are able to perform the tasks of living? A person does not know how, he just knows that he can.. Even so, through constant effort towards higher spiritual attainment,

one develops a second nature type of ability to communicate with God.

WHO IS THE HOLY SPIRIT?

According to popular religious teaching the Holy Spirit is one of the Divine Trinity, and this is true. The Holy Spirit is the active principle of universal life force which gives being to all that is in the higher and lower worlds. The Holy Spirit is also the part of God which awakens the slumbering divinity within man. However, in metaphysical terms the Holy Spirit may also be interpreted to mean "a holy spirit", or the spirit of an advanced soul or angel which may inspire and help us. In any case we can only communicate with holy spirits or the Holy Spirit as we make progress on the path which brings us to our next consideration.

THE NINE FRUITS OF THE SPIRIT

Within the pages of the Holy Bible St. Paul reveals nine qualities of character which we must conceive and nurture as we develop on the path. "But the fruit of the Spirit is love, joy, peace, longsuffering (patience), gentleness, goodness, faith, meekness (humility), temperance." Galatians 5:22,23

1. Love -- Let us consider these desired qualities beginning with love. The love spoken of here is not a selfish or personal love but a higher type of love which adores and respects all life.

2. Joy -- Joy means that we should try to keep only positive thoughts which will inspire us to happiness, so that we will attract only positive influences.

3. Peace -- Peace should be our goal that we may consider ourselves in harmony with everything and everyone.

4. Patience -- Patience is a virtue and we must keep reminding ourselves that Rome was not built in one day. Everything takes time and effort to be of any lasting value.

5. Gentleness -- Gentleness means that we should take note of how we come across to others and make that extra effort to be kind.

6. Goodness -- Goodness means that we should be kind for the sake of kindness; that we should do for others out of the goodness of our hearts.

7. Faith -- Faith is the flame which illuminates our religion. Without faith it is impossible to touch God. My advice to all is, do not try too hard to have faith: When you mail a letter you do not worry about how it will reach its destination, you simply believe that it will after you drop it in the mailbox. As you observe the visible works of God within nature it becomes easier to realize the reality of the invisible world or cause behind the effect -- it becomes easier to have faith.

8. Humility — Humility means that we should become as little children, that we may enter God's Kingdom. A child is trusting, simple and believing. We must be willing to release the carnal reasoning which hinders us from spiritual progress, and we must discard the empty pride of life which brings sorrow. To be humble is to be powerful where power counts.

9. Temperance -- Temperance means to be moderate. Many of us tend to overdo things, especially that which is not good for us. When we do all things in moderation it helps us to stay in balance and stay free from the bondage of external things.

The more we attempt to develop the nine qualities just mentioned, the closer we get to the Almighty. As we change our thoughts and feelings we begin to experience a transformation within our lives. This has been termed "Being Born Again", or "Conversion". As we build a direct link to the Holy Spirit we realize the development of certain powers, which brings us to our next consideration.

THE NINE GIFTS OF THE SPIRIT

"For to one is given by the Spirit the word of wisdom the word of knowledge faith gifts of healing working of miracles prophecy discerning of spirits tongues (speaking in tongues) interpretation of tongues. - I Corinthians 12:8--10

1. The Word of Wisdom -- This means to have a mastery of practical aspects of mystic power. To be wise in your understanding and application of divine laws within your daily life.

2. The Word of Knowledge -- This means to make it your business to know what is necessary for spiritual power. Faithful study brings knowledge and knowledge is power. The more we desire knowledge, the easier it becomes to receive it.

3. Faith -- This is the faith which is a spiritual gift, so powerful that it becomes a dynamo to generate daily miracles within your life. The Master said that faith, as a grain of Mustard Seed, could move

mountains. This means that we should concentrate our faith into a point of energy which holds the very force of the atom. The secret is: focus thoughts into positive directions towards the realization of our goals.

4. Gifts of Healing -- These are of a greater power than mental or herbal healing. Spiritual healing comes from the very core of life to remove the cause of the illness.

5. The Working of Miracles -- This means that when we blend into the all powerful will of God, good things flow easily to us and those we love. To be in universal harmony with life is to have a direct link with the source of miracles. Wise teachers have given us a hint to this secret in the words, "let go and let God".

6. Prophecy-- This is the power to foretell future events. Great prophets, such as Moses, Daniel, Ezekiel, Nostradamus and others were able to foretell the future with outstanding accuracy through the gift of prophecy. Within the mind of God is the knowledge of all that was, is and shall be. As we allow our mind to be touched by God's mind, we shall be able to use this wonderful gift.

7. Discerning of Spirits - This means to know the true character of any spirit we may be in communication with. There are evil spirits who pretend to be angels of light for the purpose of leading men astray. With this spiritual gift operating in your life, you will be able to detect a deceiving spirit. Also, let us remember that not all evil spirits are discarnate: Many people that we meet may act very nice outwardly, but actually be wolves in sheep's' clothing.

8. Speaking in Other Tongues -- Inspired speaking is a spiritual gift which enables one to speak a language unknown to the speaker, for the purpose of giving a divine demonstration to others. At times one may speak a heavenly tongue, also known as the language of angels.

9. Interpretation of Tongues -- This means that we are able to know what we have spoken in unknown tongues while inspired.

Let us remember that we must crawl before we can walk and walk before we can run. Patience, consistent effort and faith are the three main ingredients which yield success in psychic and spiritual development. Start at the bottom, work your way to the top, and believe that you shall become powerful.

There is a superior part of us which transcends our physical, emotional and mental faculties, and that is our true self, the spiritual man. Our spiritual body is the high self of our existence and is a

three fold manifestation of love, will and wisdom in their highest form. As we progress on the path we become more aware of the true self, thus becoming more aware of God, for it is this part of us that is made in the image of the Almighty.

THE MIND IS THE CRUCIBLE OF MAGIC

Let us first define the term. What is Magic? The best definition so far brought forward by the myriad of writers on this theme is: THE ART OF CAUSING CHANGES TO OCCUR IN SITUATIONS, IN CONFORMITY TO YOUR WILL.

That understanding of the word Magic brings it down to the Human level of application. One may will that a Leopard change his spots, but such a Will could never buck Dame Nature. One can, however, will that certain other people do things, or take specific courses of action, and can, by magical methods, bring such about There is mystery and wonder, magic, if you will, in the unfolding of a flower bud. that type of Magic does not depend on a Human Will.

Manipulative Magic is the work of the Human Will, as a Species. A Will built the Suez Canal, wrapped islands with pink plastic, erected the Sears Tower, etc. It did so by the application of Principles. It is the application of Metaphysical

Principles which will work the mystery we call Magic. You must produce an emotional vibration, give it intention, or "charge" it, as was said of old, and direct it by force and Will. You must produce an emotional vibration, give it intention, or "charge" it, as was said of old, and direct it by force of Will. IMAGINATION, WILL, and FAITH, the operations of which, kept secret, produces Power from the Practitioner's own mind.

You should develop the ability of a single pointed concentration and the knack of conjuring and controlling visions in the imagination. The more emotional feeling the visions are able to arouse in you, the more potent they will be in casting Spells and working Magic.

Your Will is the focusing lens through which emotionally charged vibrations pour forth from you into the atmosphere around about Hold steady to your faith in yourself and your ability in working Magic. Picture your intentions as happening and act as if the desire is in the process of coming about.

119

Keep the workings of your Magic secret from the Multitude, the Crass and the Vulgar. You use the electrical elements which flow through your own mind; id est, your own emotions and desires.

The materials and objects you use in a Spell are not magical per se. The effect they have as "symbols" in your own Subconscious, to stimulate emotional excitement and conjure the desired intention to your Mind's Eye, however, is magical.

In this respect there is no difference in what is called White or Black Magic. The power conjured and directed is in itself neutral. The only difference at all is in the intention of the one working with h. The personal "ethics" of the Practitioner, in other words. Take heed, mental doubts cause Magic to fail. Never give in to doubt Never try to reason it out. Magic is an emotional Art, not a rational one. Once you doubt, all your works come to naught.

A FEW WORDS TO THE WISE ON PSYCHISM

In the Psychic Arts, so often one must open up to the influences from the outside, such as in Mediumship. True Spiritual knowledge and Wisdom comes from the inside. Do not ever be a passive Psychic, by allowing oneself to be told what to do and how to act by any force or entity outside yourself.

They can be allowed to communicate, but not direct your actions. Be receptive to the "vibes," but also in control of yourself. Should ever a communicating Spirit make one feel uncomfortable, close the channel at once.

Beware of those that ask your permission before they can act or do anything for you. Their motives are evil. Higher Entities do not need to ask, but will never do anything contrary to your Freedom of Choice. The Lower ones do not have any spiritual authority and need your consent to act on your behalf. Send them straight away, no matter how pleasant or flattering they are to you.

If you do not control them, they will control you.

THE ART OF READING VIBRATIONS

To read vibrations from things and persons was a psychic talent much employed in the Ancient World. Priestesses, and to some degree Priests, in the Shrines of the Old Gods used these Mystic Arts to help their communities. The young person, male, but more

particularly female, was dedicated at an early age when he/she showed signs of Seership.

Heightened sensitivity was usually the key. During the time the politically oriented Christian Clergy usurped spiritual leadership in the Western World, Divination was made to be anathema, and the strict codes of the example of the Hebrew Temple in old Jerusalem, as to patriarchal authority, was used to decry "Psychic" gifts throughout Christendom.

Most, if not all, organized hierarchical religious structures hate the fluid Psychism of Priestesses. Divination and Psychism show the Spirit World and Inner Planes of Being not to be what and as the Clergy says. A Clergy's ploys for power and control of people's Minds will not impress those who know spiritual things.

Hence, the Old Religion had to be prevented from having an appeal in the hearts of the multitude. Hence, the Devil was invented and made to be "Father of Lies" with women in Psychism as his minions. Hence, the most dastardly deeds of the Christian Religion; the Witchcraft Mania.

Let us leave such a sad thought and allow Christianity to rue its own acts of hateful violence. The Old Religion resurgeth! We no longer have the Outer Porticos of the Temples to train and develop the Seers and Seeresses. However, much may still be done by one developing alone.

Begin to develop your inner awareness by meditating on your concept of the God/Goddess, Creator/Creatrix.

Anoint your throat, brow and Solar Plexus with Deja Vu, Spirit Channeling or Sandalwood Oil and burn Mugwort as an Incense when you meditate.

Go out into Nature and commune with Wind, Sea, Mountain, Desert, Farm Land, Tree, Lake, River, etc.

Feel the vibrations and the messages they have to tell you. Sit by, or in them, allowing all care to drain away and out of you. Let them fill you with their voices and feelings.

Next, drain all tension and observe people as they go about their daily fives.

Pick up what such feelings and "vibes" tell you.

Impressions from those things and persons will begin to tell you very much.

They may come to the head or to the Solar Plexus. Allow them to enter and speak to you.

Joy and Sadness, wonder and woe, experience them all.

Thirdly, take up objects from Nature and handle them. Go into yourself and try for an At-One-Ment with them. Their tales will unfold for you.

Fourthly, apply that ability to objects from persons, having been in close proximity to them for periods of time. They will unfold tales of stronger vibes.

Place the object against your forehead or Solar Plexus, quiet the mind and empty the feelings. Sense out to the object and try to connect with it.

Speak out exactly what picture comes to mind, or what feelings well up in you. Do not reason it out. If you do, the First Impressions will weaken and not be vivid and reliable.

The "Yes, but No!" Psychic is seldom valid.

Fifthly, when you presume to give "Readings" by Psychometry for others, you should burn a bit of Mugwort before hand to help open psychic channels, by breathing in the fumes.

Keep a goblet of Water at your left hand during a reading. Have a white, blue or yellow candle gently lighting the area. Thus do three of the Ancient Elements of the Wise help; Air, Fire and Water produce Earth, which is the Manifestation you would bring about, your portend or prognostication.

Scrying, Automatism and Psychometry are the three Powers of the Witches of Old. Work them well, within the bonds of good taste. Know and Beware! Your Power as a Seer will be lauded and sought after by many.

Some are impressionable and suggestible. They would want your leave to visit the restroom and would also ask your leave to flush! That places great power in your hands over them.

Unethical manipulation of others for your own ego and/or unreasonable financial gain brings you into the Realm of the Black Magician. The Lords of Karma will never be cheated!

Do not allow any to fix an unhealthy dependency on you, as a Reader, to the exclusion of common sense. What you may see in "Spirit" for your Querents is only the most logical conclusion of their present course of action, good or ill.

At any moment in Time and Space, each one may choose a different path to take, leading to a different "Future." Divination only helps one assess the Past and the Present, to be able to arrange the Future and navigate more advantageously. Let each Querent be the Captain of His/Her own Soul.

In that way, you become a Seer or Seeress in the best traditions of the Ancient Wisdom Religion of the Old Gods.

FIGHTING NEGATIVE FORCES

Curses and Hexes are not recommended for the Student of Occultism to use and bandy about unwisely. Many persons shrink from that aspect of the Occult altogether and try not to even hear about such methods. However, that puts them at a disadvantage when and if a notorious Magician of unethical means sets out to make life difficult for them.

Do not be deceived! When you begin to be a Force in Occult Studies, even for what you consider to be "good" or positive, you do and will come to the notice of certain persons of not so altruistic bent.

Cursings and Hexes are very much a part of the Occult World, no matter how much one may protest to the contrary. Some persons, albeit deluded and misguided, do cast Hexcraft for many reasons. Therefore, it is necessary to know Hexcraft in order to protect and deflect and reverse such negative works.

Occult Pollyanas, who sing hearts and flowers and swear they never engage in negative things, can and do leave themselves wide open to attacks by the unscrupulous and the Black Magician. When it becomes known that you are knowledgeable in the Occult, certain types of individuals will try to play The Wizard's Ball Game with you, just to see if you are worth your stuff.

It is usually Ego and lust for Power that distinguishes such persons. They want to impose their mark on your Psyche, to let you know you are nothing in their eyes. They seem to have a need to be known, and felt to be an imposing presence in Occult Circles. That kind of attitude leads to their eventual downfall.

How can you work against evil influences, if you do not know how it is accomplished in the first place? Contempt for others, ego-inflated desire for power, and under-estimation of another Practitioner, usually accomplish their own ruin.

A Black Magician would have such a low esteem for you, that he/she would normally not take precautions to prevent your positive magics being able to lift and send back Hexes. Black Magic is easily defeated.

Evil sorcery cannot withstand a positive confrontation for any extended period of time. Negativity is intense and works very quickly, but soon evaporates from its inability to sustain the effort.

Eventually it is overcome and absorbed into the positive background of the Cosmic Universe as a whole and becomes the compost for bigger and better things to follow. So much for evil Wizards!

A Black Magician operates on fear. The fear he/she creates for him/her self in others, and his/her own paranoia. It takes enormous effort to cause others to fear and more effort to constantly be on the defensive against the possibility of magical retaliation. A Black Magician can sustain a magical attack only on a limited scale.

He/She fights on two fronts at once and can and will be worn down by persistent and bold, sustained effort. After all, the positive Practitioner has all the energy of the Cosmos on which to call, and no time limit in which to use it.

One thing, however, you must not do, is pity the Black Magician. You must proceed against him/her relentlessly, applying positive force against negative. Negativity will always be forced to give place. That is Cosmic Law.

Maintaining a healthy frame of mind, healthy vital energy, and positive attitude and common sense self-worth, will do more to prevent an attack of Black Magic than anything else.

An evil Sorcerer will try to gain access to your inner mind by pressing on your Psychic Centers with a strong Thought-Form. If you are not in a healthy vitality, you may feel the heat or tingling sensations of something trying to invade your being.

Hold the thumbs of each hand in the center of the palms of the opposite hands. If you can, sit down and cross the feet. This position closes you off, as a contained circuit, and prevents any energy loss the Black Magician is trying to drain away.

Then silently, begin to breathe steadily and deeply to restore and charge up the aura. When you feel at peak, project that energy out and at the direction from whence the creeping evil seems to be coming. The Evil One will receive a blast not expected.

Then close off again with the thumbs and crossed feet and remain silent until the feel of the danger has drained away. The Black Magician will have to slink back to the darkness and mull over what happened.

The thumb-holding technique is age old and has been used by many Practitioners to prevent adverse energy sent by one of evil intent from gaining access into one's being.

Ritual Ablutions are another means to ward off and keep negative energies at bay. They are Ritual bathing and Spiritual Acts of Cleansing. They are a series of Ritual Immersions in Bath Water to which Blessed Salt and Herbs, either in bulk or by Essential Oil, have been added.

The metaphysical idea being that of certain scents can give a positive power to one's own vital energy, in the aura, which prevent hostile intent from the malice of evil wizards affecting one adversely.

Bath crystals scented with Wisteria, Sandalwood, Almond, Heliotrope, Jasmine or Vetivert would be ideal to use in Ritual Ablutions.

Those Herbal Scents have a correspondence to establish positive energies and lift negative psychic intent.

A Ritual Bath would entail those Bath Crystals poured into the hot bath water and total immersions, perhaps three times, for a period of about eight minutes. Meditations or prayers are said to ward off and/or lift jinxed, crossed or hexed conditions in one's life. Then one must air dry, rather than towel dry with an herbal scented bath.

One's body and aura would then have the uplifting quality of the herbal essences and act as a barrier to keep ill wishing away.

The astrological forces used to remove jinxes would be Mercury, under a waxing Moon, in an Air Sign.

On those days or nights the occult energies are much more conducive to the processes of lifting negative thoughts and/or crossed conditions put upon one by the dark intentions of an evil Wizard or Sorcerer/ess.

The nasty or evil intentions can be readily lifted and sent back to fester in the mind which conceived them. When Black Magic is properly deflected, it returns along the line of least resistance to its point of origin.

What the Black Magician had in mind for the victim manifests in his/her own circumstances. That is the just reward any abuser of the Occult Arts should receive.

A RITUAL TO REVERSE CURSES AND HEXES

3 Yellow or White Candles

1 Bottle Witchbane, Jinx-Removing or Uncrossing Oil

1 Packet Hermes Incense.

On a Day of Mercury, as Luna waxes in an Air Sign, light a bit of the Incense and say:

SPIRITS OF THE ELEMENTS OF AIR

GATHER TO THIS CENSE MOST FAIR.

DRIVE OUT ALL DEMONS OF DARKER MIEN.

DISPELL THE HATE OF GALL AND SPLEEN

Anoint the three candles with the oil and vision the intentions of all evil thought returning to the one who sent them.

Anoint also the victim upon whom the negative attack was directed on the forehead, throat and chest, to lift the evil effects.

Light one of the candles and pass it thrice around the victim's head. Then circumambulate him/her thrice with the burning incense as these words are spoken:

NIGHT BE DAY!

SEND EVIL AWAY!

COLD BE WARM!

NO EVIL SWARM!

DARK BE LIGHT!

ALL HEXEREI TAKE FLIGHT!

POWER OF THE AIR SPRITES.

REVERSE ALL ADVERSE FRIGHTS.

SEND BACK TO THE EVIL ONE,

TO HIDE FROM LIGHT OF SUN.

IT SHALL BE AS IF NO MORE,

ALL EVIL FLEE FROM THIS VERY DOOR!

Allow the candle and incense to burn themselves out.

Repeat this each day thereafter for two more days, until the three candles are gone. The delivered victim should wear the oil as a body cologne until signs of the reversal are apparent.

TO REVERSE A SPELL

3 White Candles

1 Bottle Mercury Oil

1 Packet Compelling Incense

On a Day of Mercury, as Luna waxes in an Air Sign, anoint the three candles with the oil and set them in a row to stand North to South.

Set the Incense to burn and concentrate on reversing any thought that has been conjured and sent out Light the candles from North to South and chant:

BE STOPPED! BE TURNED! BE RIGHTLY BURNED!

REVERSE THE FLOW OF SPELLS SINCE CAST!

REVERSE THE AFFECT RIGHT SMART AND FAST!

LET ALL BE TURNED TO NAUGHT AND NILL!

ONLY THE OPPOSITE MY THOUGHTS SHALL FILL!

Vision the affect of Magical Works being reversed until the candles are reduced to mere stubs. Snuff them out in reverse order of lighting; South to North.

Scatter the stubs and ashes to the Four Winds.

THE POWER OF PRAYER

Prayer is an intangible entity. It works, but we know little about it. The subject has never been fully explored, which is rather incredible. We can find plenty of examples to show that prayer works, and we can point to people like Charles Steinmetz, the electrical genius of the General Electric Company, who said that the next realm of research would be the spiritual, and the next field that of prayer.

His prediction hasn't come true yet, but Dr. Norman Vincent Peale said, "Prayer is the greatest power in the world. It is a pity that more people do not know how to use it."

Some time ago Reverend Franklin Loehr decided to find out once and for all if prayer really worked. He was a chemist as well as a theologian, and his experiment consisted of a series of tests on living plants at the Religious Research Foundation, Inc.

Altogether, Rev. Loehr conducted 700 experiments. A total of 27,000 seeds and seedlings were used, and more than 100,000 measurements were taken. Six other experimental groups supplemented and corroborated the reverend's work.

Dr. Loehr's results indicate that a thought is a thing, meaning that the brain emits waves strong enough to be measured and graphed. One group among his 150 assistants prayed to God that their seeds would be successful and healthy. Another group made no such plea to God. The seeds that were prayed over grew three to four times faster than those which received no prayer.

If prayer works well on seeds, why not us? Spiritual aid is there for the asking. It works no matter what your religious persuasion is. After all, didn't we start as seeds? Although we will pray for good health and longevity, we must remember that in our prayers the phrase must always be: "Not my will, but Thine will be done."

FIVE STEPS TO TAP THE POWER OF PRAYER

1. Relax. The room should be dark, or semi-dark, and you should be alone and with no distractions.

2. Accept or "turn on" the power of prayer, which can be had for the asking. This ability increases with practice.

3. Direct the power to what you want accomplished. This, too, will take a bit of practice because our minds tend to wander.

4. Visualize it as you want it to be. In this case we want good health and vigor into old age. Picture yourself as being healthy and vigorous even though, in your mind's eye, you may be well up in years.

5. Give thanks that it is being accomplished. We give thanks all the time to those who do small favors for us, why not extend our thanks to God for the biggest favor He can bestow on anyone— good health?

THE IMPORTANCE OF FAITH

Dr. Carl Jung once said, "In all the thousands who come to me for help, those who have some faith, some religion, get well more quickly."

Mature people are spiritual people. That doesn't mean that they follow a particular religion, but they do have faith in themselves and in others.

They are aware of the fact that there is a power greater than themselves and that the universe has a purpose as well as order.

CONTACTS WITH ASTRAL ENTITIES

Attempts at using magic often will evoke beings from different levels of reality, or astral planes. It is inevitable that these celestial creatures will be called, whether you meant to or not. Because this is unavoidable, it is best that you know what to do when an astral visitor comes calling.

Most of these astral beings were never human, and never will be, for they belong to an entirely different order of nature. These strange entities are ordinarily invisible to human beings, but under certain conditions they may be sensed by the astral vision.

Strictly speaking, these strange beings do not dwell upon the Astral at all—that is, not in the sense of the Astral as a part of space, or a place.

We call them Astral entities simply because they become visible for the first time to man, when he is able to vision on the Astral, or by means of the astral senses—and for no other reason.

So far as place, or space, is concerned these entities or being dwell upon the earth, just as do the human beings. They vibrate differently from us, that is all. They are also usually of but a microscopic size, and would be invisible to the human eye even if they vibrated on the same plane as do we. The astral vision not only senses their vibrations, under certain conditions, but also, under certain other conditions, it magnifies their forms into perceptible size.

Some of these astral entities are known as Nature Spirits, and inhabit streams, rocks, mountains, forests, etc. Their occasional appearance to persons of psychic temperament, or in whom a

degree of astral vision has been awakened, has given rise to the numerous tales and legends in the folk-lore of all nations regarding a strange order of beings, to which various names have been given, as for instance: fairies, pixies, elves, brownies, peris, djinns, trolls, satyrs, fauns, kobolds, imps, goblins, little folk, tiny people, etc., etc., and similar names found in the mythologies and legends of all people. The old occultists called the earth entities of this class by the name of "gnomes;" the air entities as, "sylphs;" the water beings as "undines;" and the fire, or ether, beings as "salamanders."

This class of astral entities, as a rule, avoid the presence of man, and fly from places in which he dwells—for instance they avoid large cities as men avoid a cemetery. They prefer the solitudes of nature, and resent the onward march of men which drives them further and further into new regions. They do not object to the physical presence of man, so much as they do his mental vibrations which are plainly felt by them, and which are very distasteful to them.

A certain class of them are what may be called "good fellows," and these, once in a while, seem to find pleasure in helping and aiding human beings to whom they have formed an attachment. Many such cases are related in the folk lore of the older countries, but modern life has driven these friendly helpers from the scene, in most places.

Another class, now also very uncommon, seems to find delight in playing elfish, childish pranks, particularly in the nature of practical jokes upon peasants, etc. At spiritualistic séances, and similar places, these elfish pranks are sometimes in evidence.

The ancient magicians and wonder workers were often assisted by creatures of this class. And, even today in India, Persia, China, and other Oriental lands, such assistance is not unknown; and many of the wonderful feats of these magicians are attributable only to such aid.

As a rule, as I have said, these creatures are not unfriendly to man, though they may play a prank with him occasionally, under some circumstances.

They seem particularly apt to play tricks upon neophytes in psychic research, who seek to penetrate the Astral without proper instruction, and without taking the proper precautions. To such a one they may appear as hideous forms, monsters, etc., and thus drive him away from the plane in which their presence may become apparent to him.

However, they usually pay no attention to the advanced occultist, and either severely let him alone, or else flee his presence—though cases are not unknown, in the experience of the majority of advanced occultists, when some of these little folk seem anxious and willing to be of aid to the earnest, conscientious inquirer, who recognizes them as a part of nature's great manifestation, and not as an "unnatural" creature, or vile monstrosity.

ARTIFICIAL ENTITIES

In addition to the non-human entities which are perceived by astral vision, or on the Astral plane—including a number of varieties and classes other than those mentioned by me, and to which I purposely have omitted reference for reasons which will be recognized as valid by all true occultists—there are to be found on the Astral, or on the earth plane by means of astral vision, a great class of entities, or semi-entities, which occultists know as "artificial entities."

These artificial entities were not born in the natural manner, nor created by the ordinary creative forces of nature. They are the creations of the minds of men, and are really a highly concentrated class of thought-forms.

They are not entities, in the strict sense of the term, having no life or vitality except that which they borrow from, or have been given by their creators. The student of occultism who has grasped the principle of the creation of thought-forms, will readily grasp the nature, power, and limitations of this class of dwellers in the Astral.

The majority of these artificial entities, or thought-forms, are created unconsciously by persons who manifest strong desire-force, accompanied by definite mental pictures of that which they desire. But many have learned the art of creating them consciously, in an elementary form of magic, white or black. Much of the effect of thought-force, or mind-power, is due to the creation of these thought-forms.

Strong wishes for good, as well as strong curses for evil, tend to manifest form and a semblance of vitality in the shape of these artificial entities. These entities, however, are under the law of thought-attraction, and go only where they are attracted. Moreover, they may be neutralized, and even destroyed, by positive thought properly directed in the way known to all advanced students along these lines.

Another, and quite a large, class of these artificial Astral entities, consist of thought-forms of supernatural (!) beings, sent out by the strong mental pictures, oft repeated, of the persons creating them— the creator usually being unconscious of the result.

For instance, a strongly religious mother, who prays for the protective influence of the angels around and about her children, and whose strong religious imagination pictures these heavenly visitors as present by the side of the children, frequently actually creates thought-forms of such angel guardians around her children, who are given a degree of life and mind vibrations from the soul of the mother. In this way, such guardian angels, so created, serve to protect the children and warn them from evil and against temptation.

Many a pious mother has accomplished more than she realized by her prayers and earnest desires. The early fathers of the churches, occidental and oriental, were aware of this fact, and consequently bade their followers to use this form of prayer and thought, though they did not explain the true underlying reason. Even after the mother has passed on to higher planes, her loving memory may serve to keep alive these thought-form entities, and thus serve to guard her loved ones.

In a similar way, many "family ghosts" have been created and kept in being in the same way, by the constantly repeated tale and belief in their reality, on the part of generation after generation. In this class belong the celebrated historic ghosts who warn royal or noble families of approaching death or sorrow. The familiar family ghosts walking the walls of old castles on certain anniversaries, are usually found to belong to this class (though not always so).

Many haunted houses are explained in this way, also—the ghost may be "laid" by anyone familiar with the laws of thought-forms. It must be remembered that these artificial entities are of purely human creation, and obtain all their apparent and mind from the action of the thought-force of their creators. Repeated thought, and repeated belief, will serve to keep alive and to strengthen these entities— otherwise they will disappear in time.

Many supernatural visitors, saints, semi-divine beings, etc., of all religions have been formed in this way, and, in many cases, are kept in being by the faith of the devotees of the church, chapel, or shrine. In many temples in oriental countries, there have been created, and kept alive for many centuries, the thought-form entities of the minor gods and saints, endowed in thought with great power

of response to prayer, offering, and ceremonies. Those accepting the belief in these powers, are brought into harmony with its vibrations, and are effected thereby, for good or evil.

The power of the devils of savage races (some of whom practically are devil-worshippers), arise in the same way. Even in the early history of the western religions, we find many references to the appearance of the

Devil, and of his evil work; witchcraft diabolical presences, etc., all of which were created thought-form entities of this kind. Many of the effects of sorcery, black-magic, etc., were produced in this way—the element of belief, of course, adding greatly to the effect. The Voodoo practices of Africa, and later, of Martinique; and the Kahuna practices of Hawaii, are based on these same principles. The effect of "charms," etc., depend on the same laws, including the effect of faith.

Even certain forms of "spirits," so-called, of certain forms of spiritualistic séances arise from this principle, and have never been human beings, at all. An understanding of this principle will aid in the interpretation of many puzzling phases of psychic phenomena.

SPIRIT RETURN

Nothing that I have said must be taken as denying the reality and validity of what the western world knows as "spirit return." On the other hand, I am fully familiar with very many instances of the real return to earth-life of disembodied souls. But at the same time, I, as well as all other advanced occultists, are equally aware of the many chances of mistake in this class of psychic phenomena. Shades, and even astral shells, too often are mistaken for departed loved ones. Again, many apparently real "spirit forms" are nothing more or less than semi-vitalized thought-form artificial entities such as I have just described.

Again, many mediums are really clairvoyant, and are able to unconsciously draw to some extent upon the Astral Records for their information regarding the past, instead of receiving the communication from a disembodied soul—in all honesty and in good faith, in many cases. Occultism does not deny the phenomena of modern western spiritualism—it merely seeks to explain its true nature, and to verify some of it while pointing out the real nature of others. It should be welcomed as an ally, by all true spiritualists.

ASTRAL VISION

It must not be supposed that the astral vision dawns suddenly upon anyone, in full force. Rather is it a matter of slow gradual development in the majority of cases. Many persons possess it to a faint degree, and fail to develop it further, for want of proper instruction. Many persons have occasional flashes of it, and are entirely without it at other times.

Many "feel" the astral vibrations, rather than seeing with the astral vision. Others, gain a degree of astral vision by means of crystal gazing, etc. That which is frequently referred to as "psychic sight," or "psychic sensing," is a form of astral visioning or sensing. Psychism is bound up with astral phenomena, in all cases.

SECRETS OF ANGELIC CONTACTS

The first step to take on the wonderful path that leads to "Higher Contact" with our Guardian Angel is this: making "X" contact. It is so important to all who are desirous of consciously communicating with these entities that I cannot overemphasize it.

What is "X"? Simply a symbol for your own highest spiritself. It is the high-self intelligence of you.

X, as we all know, is used in mathematics to stand for the "unknown factor." The unknown factor in my own life for many long and bewildering years was my Higher Self. I was like countless other persons, totally unaware of the existence of my higher self. It is exceedingly difficult—if not impossible—to become aware of one's higher self when one's ordinary human self demands all the attention.

AN ANGELIC VISITOR

In 1940, I had a most unusual and startling experience that brought me "face to face" with my unknown higher self. I was, however, a deep and serious student of the "hidden secrets" of life. My book shelf bulged with "occult" books of every description—and yet I had never touched reality.

One night after reading a chapter or two of an advanced and complicated treatise dealing with "White Magic," I turned out the light in my bedroom and went to sleep. It was my usual bedtime—ten o'clock—and sleep came quickly.

I slept for several hours. Then, at about 2:00 AM, I suddenly was aroused to full conscious awareness. Something strange and unusual was about to happen. I sensed that what was about to occur would be of deep soul significance. In a few moments my premonition was confirmed.

As I lay where on my bed in the darkness of my little room, opening both eyes to see whatever I could in the dark, it happened.

A tall, graceful being in the form of a man wearing a light flowing robe, quietly entered through a closed door and walked over to my bedside. Yes, he had walked right through the solid door and, as he stood beside me, I felt my own body begin to tremble. My eyes seemed riveted upon the remarkable being who had just "stepped into" my life in this unusual manner.

He was indeed extraordinary. Tall, well proportioned and majestic in his appearance. I had only to look into those amazing eyes of his to know, here was a being of marvellous power and intelligence. His entire body radiated a beautiful light so that I could see him easily in the dark. It seemed to me that little rays of light shone from his large eyes that sparkled like blue diamonds.

The calm expression on his face indicated perfect balance of strength and love and high intelligence. And yet—I was excited and afraid.

Why? I do not know. Perhaps fear comes too naturally, too easily to the majority of us earthlings. Maybe that is why we get into fights and yes, wars, so frequently. For me, in those early days, fear was an emotion I had not yet cast out of my consciousness.

I felt that emotion then.

The "Angel"—for such he most certainly was—had no intention of disturbing me further. At once he became aware of my fear and with a gentle, understanding smile upon his lips, turned around and was soon gone.

Then came a voice of my own higher self—soft but clear— "Be not fearful of your Teachers. Learn the lesson of higher love.

HARMONY WITHIN ALL CREATION

See harmony within all creation and build a greater realization of oneness with all living beings. In this perfect love all fear is dissolved."

That was a big lesson for me to learn. And it was not until I had really transmuted fear into the higher love that the "Brothers of the Higher Arc" could reach me and teach me other important lessons. Keep this in mind as you continue your progress as a New Age Individual seeking higher contact. Love is the realization of oneness. It is the soul's sincere desire for health, harmony and happiness within all beings.

Don't, for heaven's sake, be like me—so upset that I actually "frightened" my teacher away! When your time for meeting a marvellous angelic being arrives, by all means try to maintain your composure. There is no good reason to be afraid of any advanced being who sends out the wonderful vibration of higher love to you. On the other hand, if the "harmony vibration" is missing in your contact with any being of advanced intelligence, be careful. It is possible for us earthlings to contact advanced beings who are advanced mentally but not spiritually. My advice is to always be wary of any intelligence who is "all mind, but no heart."

It is your privilege and responsibility to "test these angelic beings" before following their suggestions or advice. How do you test them? Very simply. By the trinity principles of Power, Love and Wisdom. The Lord's angels always bring about a beautiful and "balanced" effect when they communicate with you. That is because they never over-emphasize one aspect of the trinity at the expense of the other two. When they apply Power they use an equal amount of Love and Wisdom at the same time.

This causes their thoughts, feelings and actions to be harmonious, positive and joyously constructive. No matter what Teacher you contact, either on the mental, the astral, or the physical plane, test him or her for BALANCE. If you sense inwardly that he is bringing inharmony to your soul by an imbalanced vibration, this is NOT your Guardian Angel.

A WORD OF CAUTION

Regarding all contacts with angels, a word or two of caution. Never be frivolous. Frivolity is out of place, because it indicates disrespect. Communication with angelic beings is serious and of the deepest importance to you and humanity. Reaching the mind of an angel is no simple matter. There has to be a very close "attunement" of both soul and mind before the condition of rapport is achieved between you.

Here is the basic procedure to follow:

1. Wholehearted desire. You must desire to contact your Guardian Angel with a deep-souled intensity.

2. Belief in them. You must feel in your heart that these angels exist just as you do; that they can respond to you.

3. Be sincere with yourself. Ask yourself, "Why do I desire to contact my Guardian Angel?" Purity of motive and sincerity are the attitudes that will protect you from unwanted, lower entities and vibrations. They are your "shield and buckler."

4. Raise your vibration. Body, Soul, Spirit have to be raised to a new and higher level of awareness. Your awareness must rise above earth's sphere until it reaches the High Arc of Heaven.

CONTROL OTHERS WITH PSYCHIC INFLUENCE

Psychic Influence can be divided into three general classes, (1) Personal Influence, in which the mind of another is directly influenced by induction while he is in the presence of the person influencing; (2) Distant Influencing, in which the psychic induction is directly manifested when the persons concerned are distant from one another; and (3) Indirect Influence, in which the induction is manifested in the minds of various persons coming in contact with the thought vibrations of the person manifesting them, though no attempt is made to directly influence any particular person.

Personal Influence, as above defined, ranges from cases in which the strongest control (generally known as hypnotism) is manifested, down to the cases in which merely a slight influence is exerted. But the general principle underlying all of these cases is precisely the same. The great characters of history, such as Alexander the Great, Napoleon Bonaparte, and Julius Caesar, manifested this power to a great degree, and were able to sway men according to their will. All great leaders of men have this power strongly manifested, else they would not be able to influence the minds of men. Great orators, preachers, statesmen, and others of this class, likewise manifest the power strongly. In fact, the very sign of ability to influence and manage other persons is evidence of the possession and manifestation of this mighty power.

In developing this power to influence others directly and personally, you should begin by impressing upon your mind the principles of (1) Strong Desire; (2) Clear Visualization; and (3) Concentration.

You must begin by encouraging a strong desire in your mind to be a positive individual; to exert and manifest a positive influence over

others with whom you come in contact, and especially over those whom you wish to influence in some particular manner or direction. You must let the fire of desire burn fiercely within you, until it becomes as strong as physical hunger or thirst. You must "want to" as you want to breathe, to live. You will find that the men who accomplish the great things in life are those who have strong desire burning in their bosoms. There is a strong radiative and inductive power in strong desire and wish—in fact, some have thought this the main feature of what we generally call strong will-power.

The next step, of course, is the forming of a clear, positive, distinct and dynamic mental picture of the idea or feeling that you wish to induce in the other person. If it is an idea, you should make a strong clear picture of it in your imagination, so as to give it distinctness and force and a clear outline. If it is a feeling, you should picture it in your imagination. If it is something that you wish the other person to do, or some way in which you wish him to act, you should picture him as doing the thing, or acting in that particular way. By so doing you furnish the pattern or design for the induced mental or emotional states you wish to induce in the other person. Upon the clearness and strength of these mental patterns of the imagination depends largely the power of the induced impression.

The third step, of course, is the concentration of your mind upon the impression you wish to induce in the mind of the other person. You must learn to concentrate so forcibly and clearly that the idea will stand out clearly in your mind like a bright star of a dark night, except that there must be only one star instead of thousands. By so doing you really focus the entire force of your mental and psychic energies into that one particular idea or thought. This makes it act like the focused rays in the sun-glass, or like the strong pipe-stream of water that will break down the thing upon which it is turned. Diffused thought has but a comparatively weak effect, whereas a concentrated stream of thought vibrations will force its way through obstacles.

Remember, always, this threefold mental condition: (1) STRONG DESIRE; (2) CLEAR MENTAL PICTURE; and (3) CONCENTRATED THOUGHT. The greater the degree in which you can manifest these three mental conditions, the greater will be your success in any form of psychic influence, direct or indirect, personal or general, present or distant.

Before you proceed to develop the power to impress a particular idea or feeling upon the mind of another person, you should first acquire a positive mental atmosphere for yourself. This mental atmosphere is produced in precisely the same way that you induce a special idea or feeling in the mind of the other person. That is to say, you first strongly desire it, then you clearly picture it, and then you apply concentrated thought upon it.

After you are filled with the strong desire for a positive mental atmosphere around you, you must begin to picture yourself (in your imagination) as surrounded with an aura of positive thought-vibrations which protect you from the thought forces of other persons, and, at the same time impress the strength of your personality upon the persons with whom you come in contact. You will be aided in making these strong mental pictures by holding the idea in your concentrated thought, and, at the same time, silently stating to your mind just what you expect to do in the desired direction. In stating your orders to your mind, always speak as if the thing were already accomplished at that particular moment. Never say that it "will be," but always hold fast to the "it is." The following will give you a good example of the mental statements, which of course should be accompanied by the concentrated idea of the thing, and the mental picture of yourself as being just what you state.

CREATE A STRONG, POSITIVE PSYCHIC ATMOSPHERE

Here is the mental statement for the creation of a strong, positive psychic atmosphere: "I am surrounded by an aura of strong, positive, dynamic thought-vibrations. These render me positive to other persons, and render them negative to me. I am positive of their thought-vibrations, but they are negative to mine. They feel the strength of my psychic atmosphere, while I easily repel the power of theirs. I dominate the situation, and manifest my positive psychic qualities over theirs. My atmosphere creates the vibration of strength and power on all sides of me, which affect others with whom I come in contact. MY PSYCHIC ATMOSPHERE IS STRONG AND POSITIVE!"

The next step in Personal Influence is that of projecting your psychic power directly upon and into the mind of the other person whom you wish to influence. Sometimes, if the person is quite negative to you, this is a very simple and easy matter; but where the person is near your own degree of psychic positiveness you

will have to assert your psychic superiority to him, and get the psychic "upper hand" before you can proceed further. This is accomplished by throwing into your psychic atmosphere some particularly strong mental statements accompanied by clear visualizations or mental pictures.

Make positive your psychic atmosphere, particularly towards the person whom you seek to influence, by statements and pictures something along the following lines: "I am positive to this man"; "He is negative to me"; "He feels my power and is beginning to yield to it"; "He is unable to influence me in the slightest, while I can influence him easily"; "My power is beginning to operate upon his mind and feelings." The exact words are not important, but the idea behind them gives them their psychic force and power.

Then should you begin your direct attack upon him, or rather upon his psychic powers. When I say "attack," I do not use the word in the sense of warfare or actual desire to harm the other person—this is a far different matter. What I mean to say is that there is usually a psychic battle for a longer or shorter period between two persons of similar degrees of psychic power and development. From this battle one always emerges victor at the time, and one always is beaten for the time being, at least. And, as in all battles, victory often goes to him who strikes the first hard blow. The offensive tactics are the best in cases of this kind.

A celebrated American author, Oliver Wendall Holmes, in one of his books makes mention of these duels of psychic force between individuals, as follows: "There is that deadly Indian hug in which men wrestle with their eyes, over in five seconds, but which breaks one of their two backs, and is good for three-score years and ten, one trial enough—settles the whole matter—just as when two feathered songsters of the barnyard, game and dunghill, come together. After a jump or two, and a few sharp kicks, there is an end to it; and it is 'After you, monsieur' with the beaten party in all the social relations for all the rest of his days."

An English physician, Dr. Fothergill by name, wrote a number of years ago about this struggle of wills, as he called it, but which is really a struggle of psychic power. He says: "The conflict of will, the power to command others, has been spoken of frequently. Yet what is this will-power that influences others? What is it that makes us accept, and adopt too, the advice of one person, while precisely the same advice from another has been rejected? Is it the weight of force of will which insensibly influences us; the force of will behind the advice? That is what it is! The person who thus forces his or

her advice upon us has no more power to enforce it than others; but all the same we do as requested. We accept from one what we reject from another. One person says of something contemplated, 'Oh, but you must not,' yet we do it all the same, though that person may be in a position to make us regret the rejection of that counsel.

Another person says, 'Oh, but you mustn't,' and we desist, though we may, if so disposed, set this latter person's opinion at defiance with impunity. It is not the fear of consequences, not of giving offence, which determines the adaptation of the latter person's advice, while it has been rejected when given by the first. It depends upon the character or will-power of the individual advising whether we accept the advice or reject it. This character often depends little, if at all, in some cases, upon the intellect, or even upon the moral qualities, the goodness or badness, of the individual. It is itself an imponderable something; yet it carries weight with it. There may be abler men, cleverer men; but it is the one possessed of will who rises to the surface at these times—the one who can by some subtle power make other men obey him.

"The will-power goes on universally. In the young aristocrat who gets his tailor to make another advance in defiance of his conviction that he will never get his money back. It goes on between lawyer and client; betwixt doctor and patient; between banker and borrower; betwixt buyer and seller. It is not tact which enables the person behind the counter to induce customers to buy what they did not intend to buy, and which bought, gives them no satisfaction, though it is linked therewith for the effort to be successful. Whenever two persons meet in business, or in any other relation in life, up to lovemaking, there is this will-fight going on, commonly enough without any consciousness of the struggle. There is a dim consciousness of the result, but none of the processes. It often takes years of the intimacy of married life to find out with whom of the pair the mastery really lies. Often the far stronger character, to all appearances, has to yield; it is this will-element that underlies the statement: 'The race is not always to the swift, nor the battle to the strong.' In Middle-march' we find in Lydgate a grand aggregation of qualities, yet shallow, hard, selfish Rosamond masters him thoroughly in the end. He was not deficient in will-power; possessed more than an average amount of character; but in the fight he went down at last under the onslaught of the intense, stubborn will of his narrow-minded spouse. Their will-contest was the collision of a large warm nature, like a capable human hand,

with a hard, narrow selfish nature, like a steel button; the hand only bruised itself while the button remained unaffected."

You must not, however, imagine that every person with whom you engage in one of these psychic duels is conscious of what is going on. He usually recognizes that some sort of conflict is under way, but he does not know the laws and principles of psychic force, and so is in the dark regarding the procedure. You will find that a little practice of this kind, in which no great question is involved, will give you a certain knack or trick of handling your psychic forces, and will, besides, give you that confidence in yourself that comes only from actual practice and exercise. I can point out the rules, and give you the principles, but you must learn the little bits of technique yourself from actual practice.

When you have crossed psychic swords with the other person, gaze at him intently but not fiercely, and send him this positive strong thought-vibration: "I am stronger than you, and I shall win!" At the same time picture to yourself your forces beating down his and overcoming him. Hold this idea and picture in your mind: "My vibrations are stronger than are yours—I am beating you!" Follow this up with the idea and picture of: "You are weakening and giving in—you are being overpowered!" A very powerful psychic weapon is the following: "My vibrations are scattering your forces—I am breaking your forces into bits—surrender, surrender now, I tell you!"

DEVELOP YOUR PSYCHIC DEFENCES

And now for some interesting and very valuable information concerning psychic defence. You will notice that in the offensive psychic weapons there is always an assertion of positive statement of your power and its effect. Well, then, in using the psychic defensive weapon against one of strong will or psychic force, you reverse the process. That is to say you deny the force of his psychic powers and forces, and picture them as melting into nothingness. Get this idea well fixed in your mind, for it is very important in a conflict of this kind. The effect of this is to neutralize all of the other person's power so far as its effect on yourself is concerned—you really do not destroy it in him totally. You simply render his forces powerless to affect you. This is important not only when in a psychic conflict of this kind, but also when you wish to render yourself immune from the psychic forces

of other persons. You may shut yourself up in a strong defensive armor in this way, and others will be powerless to affect you.

In the positive statement, "I deny!" you have the Occult Shield of Defense, which is a mighty protection to you. Even if you do not feel disposed to cultivate and develop your psychic powers in the direction of influencing others, you should at least develop your defensive powers so as to resist any psychic attacks upon yourself.

You will find it helpful to practice these offensive and defensive weapons when you are alone, standing before your mirror and "playing" that your reflection in the glass is the other person. Send this imaginary other person the psychic vibrations, accompanied by the mental picture suitable for it. Act the part out seriously and earnestly, just as if the reflected image were really another person. This will give you confidence in yourself, and that indefinable "knack" of handling your psychic weapons that comes only from practice. You will do well to perfect yourself in these rehearsals, just as you would in case you were trying to master anything else. By frequent earnest rehearsals, you will gain not only familiarity with the process and methods, but you will also gain real power and strength by the exercise of your psychic faculties which have heretofore lain dormant. Just as you may develop the muscle of your arm by callisthenic exercises, until it is able to perform real muscular work of strength; so you may develop your psychic faculties in this rehearsal work, so that you will be strongly equipped and armed for an actual psychic conflict, besides having learned how to handle your psychic weapons.

After you have practiced sufficiently along the general offensive and defensive lines, and have learned how to manifest these forces in actual conflict, you will do well to practice special and specific commands to others, in the same way. That is to say, practice them first on your reflected image in the mirror. The following commands (with mental pictures, of course) will give you good practice. Go about the work in earnest, and act out the part seriously. Try these exercises: "Here! look at me!" "Give me your undivided attention!" "Come this way!" "Come to me at once!" "Go away from me—leave me at once!" "You like me—you like me very much!" "You are afraid of me!" "You wish to please me!" "You will agree to my proposition!" "You will do as I tell you!" Any special command you wish to convey to another person, psychically, you will do well to practice before the mirror in this way.

When you have made satisfactory progress in the exercises above mentioned, and are able, to demonstrate them with a fair degree of

success in actual practice, you may proceed to experiment with persons along the lines of special and direct commands by psychic force. The following will give you a clear idea of the nature of the experiments in question, but you may enlarge upon and vary them indefinitely. Remember there is no virtue in mere words—the effect comes from the power of the thought behind the words. But, nevertheless, you will find that positive words, used in these silent commands, will help you to fit in your feeling to the words. Always make the command a real COMMAND, never a mere entreaty or appeal. Assume the mental attitude of a master of men—of a commander and ruler of other men. Here follow a number of interesting experiments along these lines, which will be very useful to you in acquiring the art of personal influence of this kind:

SEVEN VALUABLE EXERCISES

EXERCISE 1: When walking down the street behind a person, make him turn around in answer to your mental command. Select some person who does not seem to be too much rushed or too busy—select some person who seems to having nothing particular on his mind. Then desire earnestly that he shall turn around when you mentally call to him to do so; at the same time picture him as turning around in answer to your call; and at the same time concentrate your attention and thought firmly upon him. After a few moments of preparatory thought, send him the following message, silently of course, with as much force, positiveness and vigor as possible: "Hey there! turn around and look at me! Hey! turn around, turn around at once!" While influencing him fix your gaze at the point on his neck where the skull joins it—right at the base of the brain, in the back. In a number of cases, you will find that the person will look around as if someone had actually called him aloud. In other cases, he will seem puzzled, and will look from side to side as if seeking some one. After a little practice you will be surprised how many persons you can affect in this way.

EXERCISE 2: When in a public place, such as a church, concert or theatre, send a similar message to someone seated a little distance in front of you. Use the same methods as in the first exercise, and you will obtain similar results. It will seem queer to you at first to notice how the other person will begin to fidget and move around in his seat, and finally glance furtively around as if to see what is causing him the disturbance. You, of course, will not let him

suspect that it is you, but, instead will gaze calmly ahead of you, and pretend not to notice him.

EXERCISE 3: This is a variation of the first exercise. It is practiced by sending to a person approaching you on the street, or walking ahead of you in the same direction, a command to turn to the right, or to the left, as you prefer. You will be surprised to see how often you will be successful in this.

EXERCISE 4: This is a variation of the second exercise. It is practiced by sending to a person seated in front of you in a public place the command to look to the right, or to the left, as you prefer. Do not practice on the same person too long, after succeeding at first—it is not right to torment people, remember.

EXERCISE 5: After having attained proficiency in the foregoing exercises, you many proceed to command a person to perform certain unimportant motions, such as rising or sitting down, taking off his hat, taking out his handkerchief, laying down a fan, umbrella, etc.

EXERCISE 6: The next step is to command persons to say some particular word having no important meaning; to "put words in his mouth" while talking to him. Wait until the other person pauses as if in search of a word, and then suddenly, sharply and forcibly put the word into his mouth, silently of course. In a very susceptible person, well under your psychic control, you may succeed in suggesting entire sentences and phrases to him.

EXERCISE 7: This is the summit of psychic influencing, and, of course, is the most difficult. But you will be surprised to see how well you will succeed in many cases, after you have acquired the knack and habit of sending the psychic message. It consists of commanding the person to obey the spoken command or request that you are about to make to him. This is the art and secret of the success of many salesmen, solicitors, and others working along the lines of influencing other people. It is acquired by beginning with small things, and gradually proceeding to greater, and still greater. At this point I should warn you that all the best occult teachings

warn students against using this power for base ends, improper purposes, etc. Such practices tend to react and rebound against the person using them, like a boomerang. Beware against using psychic or occult forces for improper purposes—the psychic laws punish the offender, just as do the physical laws.

Finally, I caution the student against talking too much about his developing powers. Beware of boasting or bragging about these things. Keep silent, and keep your own counsel. When you make known your powers, you set into operation the antagonistic thought of persons around you who may be jealous of you, and who would wish to see you fail. The wise head keepeth a still tongue! One of the oldest occult maxims is: "Learn! Dare! Do! Keep Silent!!!" You will do well to adhere strictly to this warning caution.

OTHER VALUABLE BOOKS BY MARIA D'ANDREA
— ALL LARGE FORMAT WORKBOOKS · EACH INCLUDES A BONUS DVD —

( ) HEAVEN SENT MONEY SPELLS
— DIVINELY INSPIRED FOR YOUR WEALTH

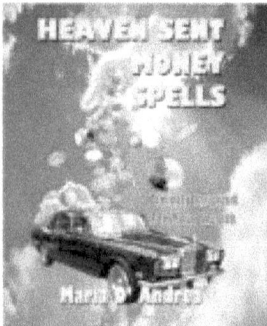

Find out why Maria is called "The Money Psychic." Imagine receiving money just by using the powers of your mind. Want a new home? Or pay off an existing mortgage?

Would you like to go on an exotic "dream" vacation with someone who is sexy or your true love? Want to sell the items laying around in your garage or attic for BIG CASH? Interested in picking a large prize lottery ticket, or winning at the tables or slot machines?

Tired of seeing someone else wearing the "Bling?" Diamonds are a girls best friend, but who cares about anyone else when that fabulous stone could be around your finger or neck?

Includes Simple Money Spells DVD— $21.95

Author And Practitioner
Maria D' Andrea

( ) YOUR PERSONAL MEGA POWER SPELLS
Includes Free 60 Minute DVD — "Put A Spell On You 'Cause Your Mine!"

Hundreds of spells that are so powerful their practitioners were once put to death for being witches. Includes spells for protection against unseen forces. Spells for love and romance. Spells for drawing the cornucopia of luck into your life. Spells for creating positive cash flow to enhance your prosperity. Spells for a healthy life. Spells for divining life's purposes with positive magick. Spells for faxing your heart's desires through meditation and visualization. — $24.00

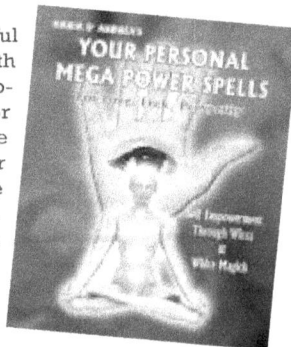

( ) OCCULT GRIMOIRE
AND MAGICAL FORMULARY

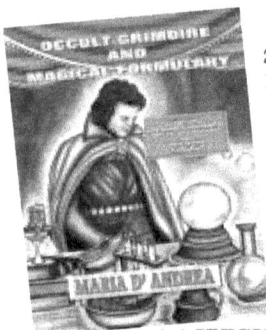

Ten books in one! – Over 500 spells! Over 200 oversized pages! With the help of this book you will learn: To manifest your own future destiny. To prevent psychic attack. To use herbal magnets. To apply candle magic to receive individual blessings. To unlock secrets of love potions. To mix the best mystical incense. To draw on the powers of crystals and stones. How prayer really works. The only true application for ritualistic oils. — $25.00

( ) SPECIAL OFFER OF THESE 3 BOOKS/DVDS BY
MARIA — $59.95 + $8 P/H

www.ingramcontent.com/pod-product-compliance
Lightning Source LLC
Chambersburg PA
CBHW050353100426
42739CB00015BB/3381